CONSCIOUS AND UNCONSCIOUS

David Edwards
and
Michael Jacobs

Open University Press

Open University Press
McGraw-Hill Education
McGraw-Hill House
Shoppenhangers Road
Maidenhead
Berkshire
England
SL6 2QL

email: enquiries@openup.co.uk
world wide web: www.openup.co.uk

First published 2003

A catalogue record of this book is available from the British Library

ISBN 0 335 20949 1 (pb)   0 335 20950 5 (hb)

Library of Congress Cataloging-in-Publication Data
CIP data has been applied for

Typeset by RefineCatch Limited, Bungay, Suffolk
Printed in the UK by Bell & Bain Ltd, Glasgow

Contents

Series editor's preface

A major aspect of intellectual and cultural life in the twentieth century has been the study of psychology – present, of course, for many centuries in practical form and expression in the wisdom and insight to be found in spirituality, in literature and in the dramatic arts, as well as in arts of healing and guidance, in both the East and West. In parallel with the deepening interest in the inner processes of character and relationships in the novel and theatre in the nineteenth century, psychiatry reformulated its understanding of the human mind, and encouraged, in those brave enough to challenge the myths of mental illness, new methods of exploration of psychological processes.

The twentieth century witnessed, especially in its latter half, an explosion of interest both in theories about personality, psychological development, cognition and behaviour, and in the practice of therapy, or perhaps more accurately the therapies. It also saw, as is not uncommon in any intellectual discipline, battles between theories and therapists of different persuasions, particularly between psychoanalysis and behavioural psychology, and each in turn with humanistic and transpersonal therapies, as well as within the major schools themselves. If such arguments are not surprising, and indeed objectively can be seen as healthy – potentially promoting greater precision in research, alternative approaches to apparently intractable problems and deeper understanding of the wellsprings of human thought, emotion and behaviour – it is none the less disturbing that for many decades there was such a degree of sniping and entrenchment of positions from therapists who should have been able to look more closely at their own responses and rivalries. It is as if diplomats had ignored their skills and knowledge and resorted in their dealings with each other to gun slinging.

The psychotherapeutic enterprise has also been an international one. There were a large number of centres of innovation, even at the beginning: Paris, Moscow, Vienna, Berlin, Zurich, London, Boston, and soon Edinburgh, Rome, New York, Chicago and California, saw the development of different theories and therapeutic practice. Geographical location has added to the richness of the discipline, particularly identifying cultural and social differences, and widening the psychological debate to include, at least in some instances, sociological and political dimensions.

The question has to be asked, given the separate developments due to location, research interests, personal differences and splits between and within traditions, whether what has sometimes been called 'psycho-babble' is indeed a welter of different languages describing the same phenomena through the jargon and theorizing of the various psychotherapeutic schools. Or are there genuine differences, which may lead sometimes to the conclusion that one school has got it right, while another has therefore got it wrong; or that there are 'horses for courses'; or, according to the Dodo principle, that 'all shall have prizes'?

The latter part of the twentieth century saw some rapprochement between the different approaches to the theory and practice of psychotherapy (and counselling), often due to the external pressures towards organizing the profession responsibly and the high standards demanded of it by health care, by the public and by the state. It is out of this budding rapprochement that there came the motivation for this series, in which a number of key concepts that lie at the heart of the psychotherapies can be compared and contrasted across the board. Some of the terms used in different traditions may prove to represent identical concepts; others may look similar, but in fact highlight quite different emphases, which may or may not prove useful to those who practise from a different perspective; other terms, apparently identical, may prove to mean something completely different in two or more schools of psychotherapy.

In order to carry out this project it seemed essential that as many of the psychotherapeutic traditions as possible should be represented in the authorship of the series; and to promote both this and the spirit of dialogue between traditions, it seemed also desirable that there should be two authors for each book, each one representing, where practicable, a different orientation. It was important that the series should be truly international in its approach and therefore in its authorship; and that miracle of late twentieth-century technology, the Internet, proved to be a productive means of finding authors, as well as a remarkably efficient method of communicating, in the cases of some pairs of authors, half-way across the world.

This series therefore represents, in a new millennium, an extremely exciting development, one which as series editor I have found more and more enthralling as I have eavesdropped on the drafts shuttling back and forth between authors. Here, for the first time, the reader will find all the major concepts of all the principal schools of psycho-therapy and counselling (and not a few minor ones) drawn together so that they may compared, contrasted and (it is my hope) above all used – used for the ongoing debate between orientations, but more importantly still, used for the benefit of clients and patients who are not at all interested in partisan positions, but in what works, or in what throws light upon their search for healing and understanding.

Michael Jacobs

Preface and acknowledgements

The words 'conscious' and 'unconscious' feature repeatedly in discussions of theory and practice in psychotherapy. Often we encounter them as adjectives: conscious thoughts and motivations are those we are aware of and can reflect on, while unconscious assumptions and motivations are those that affect our behaviour without us realizing it. Our unconscious mannerisms and expressive gestures are ones that others can see but we are quite unaware of. Sometimes we encounter these terms as nouns: 'the conscious' and 'the unconscious' are spoken of as separate domains of psychological activity; in particular, 'the unconscious' can imply the existence of potent, complex and mysterious forces at work below the surface of our conscious life, perhaps subverting or even making a mockery of our conscious understanding and definitions of ourselves. For people outside the field of psychology, the concept of 'the unconscious' may sound fascinating or even intimidating. They may look to psychologists to help them to understand or explore it. Yet many psychologists use these terms with caution or hardly at all, and would be quick to disabuse the layperson of any expectation that opening up the unconscious is something they have any interest in. The layperson might be surprised and wonder how they could have got it so wrong. Is there such a split between professional psychology and popular culture? The answer lies in what we will call 'discourse wars'. Classifying psychological activity is not as easy as classifying trees or ants. And in the complex territory of human psychology, psychologists have had trouble agreeing among themselves about what is going on. Even where they do, they may not agree on how it should be talked about. The investigation of conscious and unconscious psychological processes has a long and conflict-ridden history. Perhaps never have the conflicts been greatest than during the twentieth century.

This territory is so vast that, in planning this book, we had to make some hard choices. We give limited treatment to important related areas, which could each take up a book of their own. These include: psychological analysis of what it is to be a conscious human being, and of the centrality of that understanding to developing a comprehensive psychology (Rychlak 1997); philosophical treatments of the mind/body problem and the relationship between consciousness, mind and brain (Gray 1995; Chalmers 1996); and neuropsychological research investigating which brain pathways are associated with conscious activity and leading to detailed theories of the relationship between brain activity and consciousness (Weiskrantz 1997; Taylor 1999).

Even in the field of psychotherapy, we have addressed the work of only some of the many important theorists. In making our selection we have aimed to represent as wide a range as possible of the different kinds of position and the different kinds of discourse that have been taken up and elaborated during the course of the twentieth century. We have taken a discourse analytic approach and have presented theorists in their own words as far as possible, in order to give the reader a sense of how each one constructs the complex territory of the scope and limitations of human awareness. The book is intended to provide a kind of road map that will enable counsellors or psychotherapists to appreciate why discussions that revolve around 'conscious' and 'unconscious' can easily become so fraught with difficulty, and even, at times, the site of intense ideological struggle.

A note on terms. Within different traditions and contexts, the psychotherapist may be referred to by several terms (therapist, counsellor, analyst, psychoanalyst) and the individual with whom the psychotherapist works may be referred to in different ways too (client, patient, analysand). For consistency, we have deliberately stuck to the terms 'psychotherapist' or 'therapist' and 'client', as these seem the most neutral, except where we are quoting another writer who uses one of the other terms.

A note on citation of references. As far as possible we have indicated the original date of publication of most of the works cited. The date of the English source is noted in the reference list. Thus, for Adler (1911) the English source is 1929 but the original paper was published in 1911. In references to Freud's works, the date of first publication by Freud is indicated (e.g. Freud 1896), but our source is Freud's *Collected Works*; in the reference list we refer to the 2001 edition published by

Virago, which has the same volume and page numbers as the *Collected Works* published by Hogarth Press. Since many of Jung's papers were revised several times, often decades apart, we provide the date Jung published the version that appears in his *Collected Works*. Where we draw on Ansbacher and Ansbacher's (1958) collection of Adler's writings, we have indicated the date of the original Adler publication. Thus (Adler 1930 in Ansbacher and Ansbacher 1958: 183) means that the quoted material was published by Adler in 1930 and can be found on p. 183 of Ansbacher and Ansbacher (1958).

Acknowledgements

David Edwards would particularly like to acknowledge Claudette Kulkarni, who was initially going to co-author this book. Some aspects of the book's structure and some specific ideas contained in this book were the result of several fruitful discussions with her. He would also like to thank Rhodes University, which supported the writing of this book both financially in the form of grants from the Joint Research Committee and through providing a ten-month period of paid study leave during which much of the preparation and writing was carried out. Thanks also go to Don Maclennan for permission to include his poem 'Poems are nets of thought' in Chapter 8.

David Edwards
Michael Jacobs

CHAPTER 1

Constructing and deconstructing the unconscious

What shapes our lives and natures is not simply the content of our conscious mind, but in much greater degree that of our unconscious. Between the two is a sieve, and above is the consciousness, only the coarse material is kept back; the sand for the mortar of life falls into the depths of the It; above remains only the chaff, the good flour for the bread of life collects, down there in the unconscious.

(Groddeck 1923: 85)

As psychodynamic therapists, cognitive therapists, interpersonal therapists, and postmodern therapists maintain, there are unconscious influences on awareness.

(Rennie 2000: 165)

Psychotherapy clients usually present the therapist with intense and problematic emotions, or with vague but deep dissatisfaction, or with behaviours that are difficult to manage or out of control, or with any combination of these. They usually do not understand why they feel and behave as they do, and what understanding they do have often oversimplifies and obscures the issue. They often need help in clarifying what they are feeling, understanding the origins of their feelings and learning to tolerate painful emotional states, rather than exclude them from their awareness (Lane and Schwartz 1987, 1992). In addition, as Dostoyevsky (1868: 473) observed, 'the causes of human actions are usually immeasurably more complex and varied than our subsequent explanations of them'. This point was echoed by Baars (1997: 303) over a century later: 'We rarely have much access to the reasons why we do anything, and when we are forced to guess we are often wrong.' Furthermore, clients, like people generally, are often unaware of the impact their own behaviour has on other people, and the way this may contribute to their problems. Here, the task of the therapist is to help clients to 'see how [they are] producing [their] difficulties' (Perls 1973: 63) and so motivate and guide them to change.

In everyday life people tend to think and act as if they know a great deal more than they do about their own feelings and motives and those of others. So phenomena that point to the limits of our certainty appear somewhat mysterious or subversive of the view we have of ourselves as unitary, largely rational selves (Goldberg 1999). Since psychotherapists seek to broaden clients' awareness of themselves and their relationship to the world, it is not surprising that, in the different forms of discourse they use to discuss their work, the words 'conscious' and 'unconscious' have such a central place.

Example 1: 'I am sorry, I was not myself'

At times of emotional intensity, individuals may behave uncharacteristically. It is as if some other part of them, not in their control, suddenly takes over. In Dostoyevsky's *A Raw Youth*, Katerina, who is engaged in a deep and intimate conversation, talks about not being herself, and the narrator uses the term 'unconsciously' of her saying something that is clearly not under her conscious control:

> 'I'm a very serious person, I am one of the most serious and gloomy characters among modern women, let me tell you . . . ha–ha–ha! We'll have another talk some time, but now I'm not quite myself, I am upset . . . But at last, at last, *he* will let me, too, live in peace.' This exclamation broke from her unconsciously; I understood it at once.
>
> (Dostoyevsky 1876: 453)

Disjunction between different aspects of the self may be more dramatic: a school teacher, outwardly respectable and a role model for his pupils, reveals a very different side of himself to his therapist. Feeling deeply ashamed, he discloses 'a secret life' (Goldberg 1999: 39): he invites boys to a hotel room and has them speak to him about their lives. There is no sexual activity, but when they leave, he masturbates. In psychotherapy, clients are invited to become more conscious of the nature and roots of these kinds of inconsistencies. However, Goldberg's teacher, although in therapy (for depression), had no interest in addressing this particular behaviour. 'Unconsciousness', suggests Romanyshyn (1982: 93), 'is an absence of reflections': it is this kind of unconsciousness that the teacher wanted to maintain.

Example 2: Motivated forgetting

Freud, of course, was particularly adept at uncovering the sources of such lack of awareness. The main theme of his *Psychopathology of Everyday Life* (1901) is the way in which unpleasant emotional states, unrecognized at the time, lie behind slips of the tongue and everyday forgetting. An example, originally published by Jung, is of a man who was reciting a familiar poem but became stuck at a line about a white sheet (of snow) covering a tree. Jung asked him for his associations with the words 'white sheet' and he immediately described the following distressing thoughts and images:

> makes one think of a shroud – a linen sheet to cover a dead body
> . . . now a close friend occurs to me – his brother died recently quite suddenly – he is supposed to have died of a heart attack – he was *also* very stout – my friend is also stout and I have thought before now it might also happen to him . . . I suddenly became anxious that it might also happen [to me]; for my grandfather, too, died of a heart attack; I too am over-stout and I have therefore begun a course of slimming recently.
>
> (Freud 1901: 18)

Freud postulated that the difficulty in recalling the phrase 'white sheet' arose from 'motivated forgetting' (1901: 147) aimed at 'avoiding arousing unpleasure by remembering' (1901: 40). At the moment that it occurred, however, the origins of the man's stumbling over the words was not apparent to him or to his audience. Free association, in conjunction with the intimacy of the psychoanalytic consultation, provided Freud and his colleagues with a practical means to make a more systematic investigation of these kinds of hidden thoughts and images.

Example 3: Mary's dream

It has been recognized for centuries (see Chapter 2) that dreams may reflect aspects of our lives of which we are unaware. In *The Interpretation of Dreams*, Freud (1900) provides a detailed theory (described in Chapter 3) of how the unconscious is portrayed in the images of a dream. Faraday, whose approach is rooted in Gestalt therapy, uses a rather different approach. She describes how Mary dreamed there was something wrong with her gas stove and she needed to get it fixed. Then an explosion blew off part of the top of the stove; smoke was coming out of the burners, a hole had been burned through the wall and there was a puddle on the floor. When free association failed to yield any insight into the meaning of the dream, Faraday asked Mary to 'be the stove, to give it a voice'. Mary closed her eyes and at once started to say:

> I am a stove . . . my place is in the kitchen. People switch me on when they want to use me, and switch me off when they have finished with me . . . I'm fed up with being treated like this . . . I'm used and neglected . . . and if someone doesn't pay attention to me soon, I shall explode.
>
> (Faraday 1975: 120)

This identification exercise enabled Mary to see how the dream related to her life. She had spent much time that day supporting friends in crisis. She had lost touch with her own feelings of being taken for granted and neglected by those around her, and with the explosive anger that was building up, which could have destructive consequences. She linked the pool of water to the tears she would shed when she would eventually lose control and express herself. The hole in the wall seemed to allude to pain and tension she felt in her gut and was a warning that her unexpressed anger could give rise to physical illness.

Faraday (1975: 106) writes of how the images 'require further work before their meanings emerge', or uses the metaphor of 'unmasking dream images', so that there is an obvious continuity between Freud's observations and this kind of work. However, Faraday is cautious about referring to 'the unconscious' or activities of the 'unconscious mind', because, she says, 'the terms carry the suggestion of one or other famous theory of the nature of mind . . . people often miss important messages from their dreams by approaching them with fixed ideas about the nature of "the unconscious"' (1975: 26).

The language of the unconscious provided Freud with a tool for a pioneering investigation of human experience. However, as Freud became increasingly possessive and dogmatic about his theoretical formulations (Mullahy 1970), many later theorists were to find his use of it oppressive, serving to restrict enquiry rather than open it up. To understand this, we must look at the nature of metaphor.

As knowledge advances, language is stretched to encompass it, often by means of metaphors, which allow us 'to transfer meaning from one domain to another' (Lyddon and Alford 2000: 3). Teasdale (1996: 29) argues that there are two distinct kinds of cognitive activity, which he calls propositional and implicational. In propositional knowing, there is a fairly direct relationship between what is referred to and words that 'convey information about specific states of the world that can be verified by reference to evidence'. In implicational knowing, meaning is holistic and the truth of a statement cannot easily be directly tested by observation or experiment. Metaphor is implicational, conveying meaning in a potent manner that draws forth a complex response from the listener, by evoking frameworks of meaning that have been built up through a lifetime of cultural experience. But, being 'the language of the imagination' (Singer 1990: 12), it is inexact: its truth or accuracy cannot be assessed by specific observations.

For Freud, the concept of the unconscious drew on a spatial metaphor. He thought of 'regions' of mental activity, 'the conscious' of which we are aware, and 'the unconscious' of which we are unaware. Using this language, the unconscious is thought of as the place where the roots of a memory lapse or a depressed or hostile mood might be uncovered. These spatial connotations did not originate with Freud. In 1846, ten years before Freud was born, Carus wrote: 'The key to the understanding of the character of the conscious life lies in the region of the unconscious' (cited by Whyte 1962: 149). Even earlier, in 1758, the poet Edward Young used the metaphor of depth: 'Therefore, dive deep into thy bosom; learn the depth, extent, bias and full fort of thy mind' (cited by Whyte 1962: 111). Here self-discovery is likened to passing into a space below where we can see what is normally hidden, like the depths of a lake that cannot be seen when standing on the bank. Edward Young used another metaphor – 'contract full intimacy with the stranger within thee' – as if getting to know ourselves is like meeting someone we have never met before. Today, nearly 250 years later, these and similar metaphors are widespread in the psychological literature.

Freud was trained as a scientist and he was concerned to develop the kind of rigorous theories found in medicine and physics, which have a propositional character and need to be verifiable. Commenting on the ideas of 'the superstitious person', he argues that these are 'destined to be changed back once more by science into the *psychology of the unconscious*' (Freud 1901: 259, original emphasis). Here we see an important shift. What started as a metaphor has now taken on a propositional quality. Already, in the early part of the twentieth century, Janet had noticed this. He alienated Freud by remarking that the idea of 'the unconscious' is useful as a metaphor, but should not be made into an entity in its own right, as Freud had done (Watson 1968).

Example 4: Mrs Oak

In the last two examples, we see how free association, or identification with a dream figure, can bring hidden painful feelings into consciousness. In the work of Carl Rogers, we find a focus on the emergence into awareness of new, expanded modes of experiencing and possibilities for more effective and healthy functioning. A classic illustration of this is his description of a session with 'Mrs Oak'. During the session, she says:

> I caught myself thinking that during these sessions, uh, I've been sort of singing a song. Now that sounds vague and uh – not actually singing – sort of a song without any music. Probably a kind of poem coming out – there just seems to be this flow of words which somehow aren't forced – it sort of takes form of a . . . maybe you're just making music – I really like this – call it a poignant feeling, I mean – I felt things that I never felt before. I *like* that too.
>
> (Rogers 1967: 79–80)

In speaking of singing and poems, Mrs Oak draws on metaphors to communicate her experience. While Rogers (1951: 4) acknowledges Freud's contribution in bringing to light the 'unconscious strivings and complex emotional nature' of human beings, he develops his own distinctive discourse to articulate the dialectical process around what is and is not in awareness; and how what is currently out of awareness can emerge into awareness. This centres on terms like 'awareness', 'movement', 'experience' and 'potential self'. Mrs Oak at first doubted the value and authenticity of this new experience because it did not fit with her expectations of how she ought to be. Rogers explains that psychotherapy facilitates the development of a new kind of 'organismic awareness' by helping clients to stop trying to impose a formulation of self upon their experience, denying to awareness those elements that do not fit. He speculates that this process occurs 'at an unverbalized level in all successful cases' (Rogers 1967: 79, 80, 81).

We find an echo of this in Medard Boss (1977: 48; see our Chapter 4), who uses phrases like 'unlived possibilities' or 'unrealized existence'. In discussing the process of experiential psychotherapy, Gendlin (1996: 15) also expresses the sense of hidden potentials opening to view: 'Every experience and event contains implicit further movement. To find it we must sense its unclear edge.' In focusing on processes of awareness rather than on content, Rogers pioneered a form of phenomenological investigation of the way in which moment to moment awareness can be transformed. This is a discovery about the limits of our everyday awareness that is every bit as significant for psychotherapy as Freud's discovery of motivated forgetting.

Example 5: Kekulé s dream

Formative and creative processes may also occur in dreams. In 1865, Kekulé, a German chemistry professor, had made many fruitless attempts to map the molecular structure of benzene. Wrestling with the problem, he sat by a fire and dozed. He was accustomed to visualizing the atoms that made up the molecule, and as he dozed, he saw them again:

> My mental eye could now distinguish larger structures, of manifold conformations; long rows. Sometimes more closely fitted together; all twining and twisting in a snake-like motion. But look! What was that? One of the snakes had seized its own tail and the form whirled mockingly before my eyes.
>
> (Broughton 1986: 470)

Waking with a start, he realized the meaning of the image. All molecules mapped to date had been in the form of a linear chain. But benzene was a ring. Now he could map the atoms that made up the benzene molecule, and this led to the mapping of a whole range of other molecules with ring structures.

Artists have also received whole poems (Coleridge), musical compositions (Tartini) or the plots of novels (Robert Louis Stevenson) while they slept (Broughton 1986). Experiences like these, of creative processes, which lie outside the range of deliberate conscious thought and even waking thought, may also call forth the language of the unconscious. They may be attributed to the activity of 'the unconscious mind', which is thought of as an active, creative force with its own initiative and momentum.

Example 6: Expressive arts therapy

The expressive arts therapies directly stimulate these kinds of creative processes. Natalie Rogers, Carl Rogers's daughter, conducts multimodal workshops in which participants are invited to express themselves freely through a range of activities that include dance, drawing, painting, sculpting clay and writing about their experience. A woman called Marcia, who took part in a series of these workshops, later wrote of her experiences in a passage that includes a spontaneous use of a spatial metaphor:

> I was in no way prepared for the transforming power of art. I am not 'fluent' in art – and yet I was able to express myself most satisfactorily . . . There was so much damage to overcome, so many scars that needed to fade. The safe environment created a space . . . to venture forth into the depth of my experiences.
>
> (Rogers 1999: 117)

Art therapists often describe how people working with clay or paint feel as if some hidden hand is guiding them, or some invisible force taking over. Thus, the same woman Marcia describes how, in working with clay, 'I experienced the figures emerging without plan or thought.' Later, in reflecting on or dialoguing with the figures, their meaning becomes clear and a healing process is set in motion.

The British psychoanalyst Bollas (1987: 282) uses the evocative phrase 'unthought known' to articulate the source of what is expressed in this way (see Chapter 5): 'The dancer', he writes, 'expresses the unthought known through body knowledge.' Natalie Rogers (1999: 125–30) uses several metaphors to communicate about her work. She refers to 'accepting the shadow . . . discovering unknown parts . . . long-lost sub-personalities', and embracing 'disowned aspects of ourselves'. But, unlike her father Carl, she is also drawn to the language of the unconscious because it seems to capture the mysterious and extraordinary quality of these kinds of experience: 'The expressive arts . . . lead us into the unconscious and allow us to express previously unknown facets of ourselves, thus bringing to light new information and awareness.' As we shall see, this is very much Jung's concept of the unconscious.

Example 7: The Hillside Strangler

While he was still at school, Kenneth Bianchi may have unwittingly expressed an unknown facet of himself when he carved a sculpture of a Janus head with two faces, one of a normal person, the other of a monster. However, although he was to report having had repetitive nightmares as a child from which he would wake up screaming, to those who knew him there did not appear to have been anything monstrous about him. Then in 1979 he was arrested for a series of rapes and murders committed in the Los Angeles area by 'The Hillside Strangler'. The police had incontrovertible forensic evidence linking him to several of the crimes; yet to his employers, friends and common-law wife, he had shown no signs of being the kind of person who could commit sadistic acts. They could not believe it when he was arrested and Ken himself claimed that he had no knowledge of any of the crimes. Of course, he might have been lying, but Watkins, who examined him extensively in prison, believes that Bianchi was a multiple personality who suffered from dissociative identity disorder. Using hypnosis he contacted another part of Ken, who identified himself as 'Steve' and who freely displayed the kinds of cruelty and hostility that might be expected in a serial killer. 'Steve' willingly and accurately described the murders of which Bianchi was accused. Later, Watkins administered the Rorschach test to Bianchi twice, first while 'Steve' was 'in control' and then after Ken had been reactivated. Erika Fromm, an expert to whom Watkins sent the responses for a 'blind' interpretation', writes as follows about Ken's responses:

> relatively normal . . . quite introverted and somewhat egocentric; but all of this is within the normal range. He has good reality orientation, his thinking is logical and orderly, he seems to have good relations with other human beings notwithstanding the mild egocentricity.
>
> (Watkins 1984: 76)

By contrast, she describes Steve's Rorschach as

> one of the sickest Rorschach's I have seen in ... more than 40
> years. It is clearly that of a patient in whose mind sexuality and
> violent aggression against women are fused. I would expect him
> to be a rapist and a killer ... He can be carried away by his own
> fantasies to the point where he loses all judgement and reality
> orientation.
>
> (Watkins 1984: 77)

In cases like this there is a radical disjunction of consciousness. Ken
was completely unaware of Steve's existence.

Dissociative identity disorder is one of the starkest examples of
absence of self-knowledge, since without being aware of it the same
individual has 'two or more distinct identities or personality states
that recurrently take control of behavior' (American Psychiatric
Association 2000: 526). The person behaves dramatically differently
in the different states; for example, speaking in a different voice,
using a different vocabulary, displaying different general knowledge
and going by a different name. There are disturbances of memory,
so that when one identity is activated, there may be no access to
memories of what occurred when another identity was in charge.
Such cases have been described for over 150 years (see Chapter 2).
However, several experts at Bianchi's trial argued that he was
not a multiple personality, and some theorists believe that the
apparent dissociations that are observed are often artefactual
(Frankel 1994).

Example 8: Linda's forgotten childhood memory

It is now recognized that severe trauma in childhood plays a causal
role in the development of most, if not all, cases of dissociative
identity disorder, with its dramatic dividing of consciousness
(Putnam 1989). Throughout much of the nineteenth century, it was
recognized that forgotten childhood experiences can be a source of
psychological and behavioural problems (see Chapter 2). A comprehensive report documenting the widespread sexual abuse of
children was published by a French law professor in 1857 (Browne
1990). Freud initially embraced this view enthusiastically, and used
hypnosis and recovery of memory as a means of treatment. But
within a few years he had turned his back on the approach and cast

doubt on the validity of *some* of the childhood memories of trauma he encountered. Although his stance had enormous influence, there is increasing evidence that Freud's shift was related to strong social pressure against him (Masson 1985; Browne 1990).

Hypnosis and age regression continue to be standard practice within some contemporary approaches to psychotherapy. Dowd gives the example of a woman called Linda, who entered treatment because of fear of the dark, excessive vigilance about her safety at night and awakening from sleep screaming. Under hypnosis, she was asked to imagine the pages of a calendar flipping back a year at a time until she came to a year of special significance. This led to her recalling how, at the age of three, 'an older cousin would take her into the cellar, turn off the light, and proceed to terrify her. She would then run up the stairs screaming . . . When she came out of the trance, she stated that the cellar memory was new to her' (Dowd 1992: 280).

Dowd (1992: 215), a cognitive therapist, distances himself from Freud's concept of the unconscious, with its connotation of being a 'separate part of the mind', which he sees as a term 'loaded with conceptual baggage' (Dowd 2000: 143). George Frankl, by contrast, is quite comfortable with Freud's classic language; he considers hypnotic age regression 'a more effective highway to the unconscious than free association'. He uses the familiar spatial metaphor, observing that it provides a means to 'fairly quickly enter into the unconscious areas of the psyche, which can be considered to be the roots of the patient's disturbances' (Frankl 1994: 95–6).

In his hypnotic routine, Dowd (2000: 124) is quite willing to use the phrase 'unconscious mind' as a metaphor that will appeal to the client: 'So your conscious mind, which you use to pay attention, can take a vacation, can step aside and let your unconscious mind take over.' However, for the development of theory, which calls for a propositional language, he prefers to use terms like 'tacit knowledge' and 'implicit learning', which come from contemporary cognitive science (see Chapter 6).

We now know that trauma memories may be only partially pro-cessed, and, as a result, can give rise to paradoxical experiences. They may be entirely forgotten and recovered only during psychotherapy, or due to a triggering situation much later in life that acts as a cue to the original memory. They may also appear as intrusions of dis-sociated material, as in post-traumatic flashbacks that occur during waking or in dreams (Brewin and Andrews 1998; Andrews *et al.* 2000). While many theorists speak of the memories as 'unconscious' or 'in the unconscious', these phenomena call forth a variety of different phrases in those trying to describe and discuss them. Browne (1990), for example, refers to 'unexperienced experience'.

Example 9: The unconscious life of the world between us

Trauma memories can be thought of as 'inside us', but many theorists point out that a great deal of unconscious influence comes from outside us, from the physical and social world in which we are embedded. Thus, Romanyshyn avoids speaking of 'the unconscious', with its connotations of a 'subterranean layer', and prefers to talk of 'unconsciousness' or 'the unconscious life', which he situates in 'the world between us' (Romanyshyn 1982: 93). Many theorists address the way in which our behaviour is silently shaped by unspoken rules and norms, which are part of the structure of the wider society. Layton (1999) writes of the 'normative unconscious' as something that is 'around us' and 'between us', and can only be understood in terms of the relationships people have with others, with the culture and with the world at large. She illustrates this with a stark example. A boy phones his father. As he speaks about some upsetting things that have just happened to him, he starts to cry. His father says to him, 'Pull down your pants.' The boy does so. The father says, 'What is between your legs?' 'A penis,' says the boy. 'Yes,' says the father, 'a penis. Stop sobbing and behave like a male.' We can think of the rule that 'boys don't cry' as internalized within this machismo father, and see this harsh lesson as the way in which the father acts to ensure that it becomes internalized in his son. For Layton, however, this is far more than a dyadic transaction. The father's behaviour is part of a wider social phenomenon. Layton also uses the term 'heterosexist unconscious' to point to the complex web of actions by large groups of people, of role models in the media and of the very language we use, all of which allow unquestioned assumptions about sex roles silently to determine behaviour (see Chapter 5).

In a similar way, behaviour is silently shaped by interpersonal power relations. Thus, social psychologists Bargh and Chartrand (1999: 473) write of:

> the boss who finds his secretary attractive and believes this to be entirely due to her appearance and personality, completely unaware of the role played in his attraction by his relative power over her ... This boss would not at all be attracted by the same

woman if she were not his secretary, and he had encountered her instead in the corner coffee shop.

Like Freud, Bargh and Chartrand (1999: 462) believe that, 'most of a person's everyday life is determined not by their conscious intentions and deliberate choices'. Like Layton, they recognize that our behaviour is significantly under the control of relational factors like these unspoken power relations that 'operate outside of conscious awareness and guidance'. However, like many of the theorists we have already discussed, they do not discuss this in terms of 'the unconscious'. In fact, they carefully avoid the term 'unconscious' altogether, writing instead of 'nonconscious processes'. We see here another example of how psychologists from different perspectives share similar insights, but use different language to situate their understanding.

Example 10: The Malelukan pig goddess

Perhaps the most controversial theory of unconscious influence is expressed in Jung's (1942) idea of the collective unconscious. He observed symbols in dreams or hallucinations that had their origins in other cultures, and where it seemed unlikely that the individuals concerned had ever been exposed to them in their own cultural experience. He believed that the collective unconscious exists independently of individuals or the social processes in which they are embedded (see Chapter 3). Many contemporary psychologists would agree with Frederick Bartlett (1932: 292), a pioneer of cognitive psychology, who concluded that 'the hypothesis of a collective unconscious is completely lacking in proof'. Contemporary trans-personal theorists are more open to Jung's view. Mintz (1983: 32) writes of 'whatever deep level of the unconscious mind is psychically in touch with other individuals and perhaps with the entire universe'. Speaking from extensive experience with altered states of conscious-ness induced by psychedelic substances such as LSD, Stanislav Grof believes that Jung was right and offers an example. During the early part of Grof's career, in Prague, a man being treated with LSD-assisted psychotherapy had a vision of 'an ominous entrance into the under-world guarded by a terrifying pig-goddess'. He began drawing intricate geometrical designs, and became frustrated because he could not get the design right. Despite long discussions with the man, Grof could make no sense of this material. Years later, in the USA, Grof met

Joseph Campbell, who immediately recognized 'the Devouring Mother Goddess of the Malelukans in New Guinea' (Grof 1998: 19, 20), who had the head of a pig and guarded an intricate labyrinthine design at the entrance to the underworld. The Malelukans believed that they must be able to reproduce this design if they were to be able to pass successfully into the underworld after death.

Communities of discourse and the construction of knowledge

The examples we have described cover a range of experiences, many of which point to the limits of our everyday awareness. In the development of theories about them, we find two different processes. First, different theorists with similar insights use different terms to speak about the same kind of phenomena. For example, we found Dowd preferring to speak of 'tacit knowledge' where Frankl talks about 'the unconscious' (Example 8, p. 10). Second, theorists may address different kinds of phenomena altogether, yet use the same or similar language. Thus, we find theorists referring to 'the unconscious' when referring to emotionally painful associations, traumatic memories, emerging potential and universal and mythic images.

A constructivist approach sees knowledge building as a social process in which discourses evolve and knowledge is constructed by a group of individuals interacting with each other (Lyddon and Alford 2000). Participants in the process work together to expand and develop their ways of formulating what is discovered. There is ongoing feedback between them that allows the emergence of consensus, as some concepts or propositions find affirmation from the group, and others are revised or discarded. It is also to some extent a process of negotiation and struggle, as participants strive to promote particular concepts and ideas at the expense of others. We call the coming together of individuals within this process a 'community of discourse'.

In the development of clinical psychology and psychotherapy there has not been a single community of discourse. This is the source of many of the disagreements about how to name the phenomena we are addressing in this book. Sometimes separate communities evolve because of geographical separation. Frequently, however, ideological struggles within a community are resolved by one group leaving the community and setting up an alternative discourse. The new community develops its own infrastructure of study groups, journals, conferences and referees for resolving disputes. This fragmentation of discourse communities has been a frequent occurrence in the history of psychotherapy. As a result, we find a confusing array of competing discourses, all addressing the same spectrum of phenomena.

In the chapters that follow we examine more closely the kinds of discourse conflicts we have introduced here. But, just as importantly, we draw attention to the process of rapprochement between competing discourses that has been taking place since the 1990s. One aspect of this has been the psychotherapy integration movement (Stricker and Gold 1993). Theorists involved in this have been concerned to recover the commonalities between different theories and practices and to understand where apparent differences may represent complementarity rather than conflict. The examples in this chapter, together with further concepts and perspectives that are introduced later in the book, may provide a deconstructive toolkit that will enable the reader to step back from identification with a particular theory, and to find a way to navigate through the multiplicity of discourses that still characterize the field of psychotherapy at the start of a new century and a new millennium. But first we too step back from recent history. In the next chapter we examine the development of psychological discourses about consciousness and the unconscious up to the beginning of the twentieth century.

CHAPTER 2

Conscious and unconscious in historical perspective

If you are in search of the higher consciousness, you should study the ways of the mind ... The parade of thoughts, or concepts, or 'mental objects', through the mind is endless and infinitely complex and varied ... you will find that the mind is the source of all actions and all human states. Yet you have little positive control over [it].

(Ancient Buddhist texts, quoted in Rice 1981: 56, 111)

The key to the understanding of the character of the conscious life lies in the region of the unconscious.

(Carus 1846, quoted in Whyte 1962: 149)

Although, the terms 'unconscious' and 'unconscious mind' only began to be used in European thought from the seventeenth century, there is nothing new in the recognition that significant mental processes take place out of conscious awareness. A central focus of the teaching of Gautama Buddha (*b*. 563 BCE) was that we can significantly increase our awareness of our psychological processes through a meditative practice called 'mindfulness'. His teaching included something more radical: that systematic practice can lead to a state of *vipassana* or insight into how experience is constructed from moment to moment. Until this insight is gained, individuals are deluded about the true nature of things. A legend tells how Vipassi observes that people's 'eyes are bedimmed with dust'. However, he is able to find some 'whose eyes were not covered with dust' and when he explained the teaching to them, they told him that it was as if 'someone had ... revealed what was hidden and brought light into darkness' (Swami

Venkatesananda 1982: 14–15). Such stories and metaphors point both to the great limitations of our everyday awareness and to the possibility of expanding it significantly.

European classical literature similarly observes the value of self-knowledge at greater depth than the obvious. On the temple of the sun god Apollo, bringer of light, at Delphi, the words 'Know yourself' have inspired many, including Freud. Many of the Greek philosophers taught that only by knowing ourselves, our desires and emotions, and our patterns of thinking can a balanced life be found. Plato (428–348 BCE) suggested that getting in touch with hidden wisdom was a process of remembering something we already know but have forgotten. Plotinus (204–70 CE), who elaborated Plato's ideas, claimed that it is possible to cultivate 'another way of seeing which everyone has, but few use', and thus see into aspects of our nature of which we are normally unaware. He envisaged a 'great chain of being', a hierarchical order of existence, within which human beings are situated between the angels and the animals. This expresses the way in which both the angelic and the animal aspects of human nature are, in contemporary terms, unconscious. In turn, influenced partly by Plotinus, Augustine (354–430 CE) wondered at the 'fields and vast palaces of memory' from which a scene can arise into awareness, often 'on demand' and then sink back out of awareness again. Confronting the complexity of his own psychological processes, he remarked, 'I find my own self hard to grasp' (Chadwick 1991: 185, 193).

The French essayist Montaigne (1533–92) articulated the value of reflection on one's own psychological states and processes. His essays, considered to be the first literary self-portrait, provide reflections on, and 'experimentation with', a range of psychological experiences 'as an attempt to determine how these states of mind work' (Coleman 1987: 116). If people would observe themselves, he concludes, 'they would find themselves, as I do, full of inanity and nonsense. Get rid of it I cannot, without getting rid of myself. We are all steeped in it, one as much as another; but those who are aware of it are a little better off – though I don't know' (Frame 1955: 147). An obvious example of this self-reflection is Shakespeare's Hamlet; Shakespeare was influenced by Montaigne, and the immense literature exploring Shakespeare's characters (including from a psychoanalytic perspective) is a testimony to the power of his own self-reflection.

It is around this time, the sixteenth and seventeenth centuries, that important shifts took place, which provided the foundation for the new spirit of scientific enquiry. For example, Descartes (1596–1650), a brilliant mathematician, played a central role in developing a conceptual foundation for the natural sciences. After several years of self-questioning, he resolved to devote his life to the pursuit of scientific truth. This decision followed a series of dreams (Fancher 1979). In one, a harsh wind, which was not affecting anyone else, blew him violently against the wall of a college chapel. Did this perhaps express the conflict he felt about the pursuit of science under the shadow of the authority of a powerful church? His next dream, of a thunderstorm, reflected the intensity of his inner turmoil. In the third dream there were two books, a dictionary and a book of poetry. Descartes recognized that the dictionary represented the systematic knowledge of science, while the poetry book represented philosophy and wisdom, and a line from a poem indicated that 'the Spirit of Truth . . . wanted to open to him the treasures of all the sciences' (Whyte 1962: 89).

There are three broad approaches to understanding the relationship between conscious experience and the physical domain of the body and the world around it. The first, the materialist solution, assumes that physical matter is fundamental. Conscious experience has no independent existence but somehow arises when the physical becomes organized in specific complex ways (as in brains in general and in human brains in particular). The second, the idealist solution, supposes that what exists fundamentally is some form of consciousness, an intelligent creative source of which the material world is but a manifestation. Everyday consciousness is, then, a reflection of a deeper transcendent consciousness. The third is the solution that Descartes adopted. It involves a dualist ontology in which there are two fundamental and completely different kinds of things: the extended material world (*res extensa*); and the mind, which is the source of consciousness and thought, and which is not extended in space (*res cogitans*). Descartes believed that they interacted with each other at the pineal gland.

This dualism resulted in many contradictions when he applied it to psychological problems (Fancher 1979). However, several factors contributed to its enormous influence. At first glance, it seems to fit the facts of our ordinary perception of ourselves as a centre of experience and of a world upon which this self looks out. Further, the collapse of feudalism and the emergence of the 'modern' nation state gave a central role to enterprising economic activity and the advancement of scientific knowledge. This called for the cultivation of 'an increasingly bounded, masterful self' (Cushman 1990: 600). *Res cogitans* came to be associated not just with conscious thought, but with the self-aware, self-determined individual (Whyte 1962). Further, by separating *res extensa* from *res cogitans*, Descartes offered a solution to the conflict between the scientists and the church. The material world could be explained in terms of mechanistic principles which it was the task of science to investigate and map mathematically. *Res cogitans*, on the other hand, was not the province of science and should be left to poets and theologians.

Imagination, creativity and the invisible world

Pascal's (1623–62) remark that 'the heart has its reasons, which reason knows not' (Whyte 1962: 91) was an early critique of this new discourse, which centred on a conscious heroic self, inhabiting a world of inert physical matter. *Res cogitans* was the realm of consciousness, but it increasingly became the realm of the kind of rational thought upon which science was founded; and it provided no place for the source of that thinking, and certainly not for the creative processes of imagination and symbolism that had manifested in Descartes's dreams. Although there were attempts to incorporate the imagination as a creative element into science, these were quickly marginalized (Keller 1985). Science mistrusted imagination as the thin end of a large wedge that would legitimize superstition, and hence undermine its goals. Whyte argues that this simplistic and idealized elevation of the conscious life led, over the next decades, to the term 'unconscious' being used with increasing frequency. In 1675, Malebranche wrote, 'the awareness we have of ourselves does not perhaps reveal to us more than the smaller part of our being'; and in 1690 Norris observed, 'we may have ideas of which we are not conscious' (Whyte 1962: 96–7).

From classical times, imagination referred not to the arbitrary recombining of previous experience but to a creative force with a spiritual quality that transforms the nature and capacity of everyday consciousness and energizes the life of the soul (Singer 1990). For the poets of the Romantic movements in Europe and the transcendentalists in America, imagination was the vehicle through which the divine makes its appearance in everyday life. It was

concerned with the central issues of being ... [it] sees things to which the ordinary intelligence is blind and is intimately connected with a special insight or intuition ... [it] uncovers the reality masked by visible things ... [and] fashions shapes which display these unseen forces at work . . . [for the] invisible powers which sustain the universe work through and in the visible world.

(Bowra 1961: 5–13 *passim*)

For Keats (1795–1821), this interpenetration of the ordinary world and the life of the imagination makes the world into a 'vale of soul-making'.

In due course, the language of imagination began to converge with the language of unconscious processes. Coleridge (1772–1834) spoke of the 'twilight realms of consciousness' and articulated the 'subtle interplay between conscious and unconscious in artistic creation'. For Goethe (1749–1832), the Romantic imagination arises from 'the unconscious', which is where a person's 'root lives'. 'Poetry sets out from the unconscious', wrote Goethe's friend, the poet Schiller (1759–1805), who, a century before Freud, 'advised a friend to release his imagination from the restraint of critical reason by employing a flow of free associations' (Whyte 1962: 128, 129, 134).

In the area of dreams too, the language of the unconscious replaced the language of imagination. Descartes understood imagination to be the creative source of his dreams. Even earlier, Paracelsus (1493–1541), the German physician, had written that dreams disclose 'the shadow of such wisdom as exists in us, even if, while awake, we may know nothing about it' (Faraday 1975: 19). The Swiss writer Amiel was the first person to use the equivalent of 'unconscious' in French (in 1860), recognizing that dreams serve as a 'reflection of the waves of the unconscious life in the floor of the imagination'. In Germany, I. H. Fichte (1796–1879) referred to an 'unconscious, but rich and indeed inexhaustible background . . . [to] our clearly conscious mental life'; and how 'the depth of its range' and its 'hidden treasures' could be discovered by examining moments of insight and dreams (Whyte 1962: 156, 159).

Aspects of the unconscious: literature, philosophy and science

Numerous commentators on literature and the arts have pointed out how painting, drama, poetry and the novel bring to light aspects of human life of which we normally have limited awareness. Shakespeare is often described as standing out like a beacon of consciousness because of his ability to articulate the nuances of psychological experience and conflict. This kind of literary exploration gathers momentum from the eighteenth century onwards, as novelists and playwrights such as Jane Austen (1775–1817), Charles Dickens (1812–70), George Eliot (1819–80), Fyodor Dostoyevsky (1821–81) and Henrik Ibsen (1828–1906) used characters and situations to explore such factors as the significance of dreams, the complexity and tortuousness of hidden mental processes and conflicts between the respectability demanded by society and the impulse for free emotional expression. In a charming example of the recognition of the role of psychological conflicts in causing depression, one German novel published in 1785 portrays the practice of the 'cure of souls'. The village pastor is called to see a young woman suffering from a 'peculiar kind of depression'. He walks with her in the garden, and talks first about the love of God and then about 'the drive of the lover to be united with the beloved'. She at once tells him she is in love with a young man and confesses that she has had some sort of forbidden contact with him. The story has a happy ending: the pastor speaks to the parents, the couple are allowed to marry and the symptoms resolve! (Ellenberger 1970: 43–4).

Philosophers also explored the nature of human passions and motivations and the meaning of dreams in ways that anticipated ideas which would become prominent in the thinking of Freud and his contemporaries. As early as 1814, von Schubert's *The Symbolism of Dreams* examined the special features of the 'picture language' of dreams and recognized that dream material often has 'an amoral or demonic character because the neglected, repressed and strangled [*vergewaltigte*] aspects come to the fore' (Ellenberger 1970: 206). Schopenhauer (1788–1860) refers to the drive for sex and repro-duction as the 'unconscious will in nature' and speaks of how the 'relation of the sexes ... is really the invisible central point of all action and conduct [which] peeps out everywhere in spite of the veils thrown over it ... Sexual passion is the kernel of the will to live' (Burston 1986: 134, 143). Freud recognized that he was not the first to observe how 'a defensive striving against pain can lead to forgetting'. He quotes Nietzsche (1844–1900): ' "I did this", says my Memory. "I cannot have done this", says my Pride, and remains inexorable. In the end – Memory yields' (Freud 1901: 147). In Germany in par-ticular, the concept of 'the unconscious' gained wide popular appeal. Carus's *Psyche*, published in 1846, distinguished between different levels of the unconscious. This was a significant source for von Hartmann's *Philosophy of the Unconscious*, which discussed an absolute unconscious, a physiological unconscious and a psychological unconscious. Von Hartmann's book went through nine editions between 1869 and 1884 and the twelfth edition was published post-humously in 1923 (Ellenberger 1970; Klein 1977; Schultz and Schultz 2000).

There was also considerable discussion among philosophers such as Leibniz (1646–1716) and Kant (1724–1804) of the hidden constructive processes that form the basis for our everyday experience of the world. J. G. Fichte (1752–1814) used the term 'apperception' for these processes, which he located in 'the unconscious' (Whyte 1962: 120). Herbart (1776–1841) introduced the concept into psychology. He wrote of the building up of an 'apperceptive mass', a complex and organized structure that provided the foundation for the meanings we give to whatever we encounter in life, and the framework into which new knowledge is absorbed (Burston 1986). In 1847 Whewell conceptualized these inferential processes in terms of 'unconscious syllogism': 'sensation' (i.e. sensory information) was a minor premise; an 'idea' (the underlying organizing structure) was the major premise; and the 'conclusion' was the experience of perception. Fechner (1801–87) 'compared the mind to an iceberg which was mainly below the surface and moved by hidden currents' (Whyte 1962: 160), and applied this view to psychophysics. Helmholtz (1821–94) is known for his emphasis on 'unconscious inference' in perception (Fancher 1979). In 1862, on the basis of his experimental studies, Wundt (1832–1920) concluded that the 'assumption of unconscious logical processes correctly declares the real nature of [perceptual] processes, although the processes themselves are not accessible to immediate observation' (Burston 1986: 135).

Approaches to somatoform and dissociative psychopathology

In medicine the concept of imagination, which had long been invoked to explain a wide range of psychological and behavioural symptoms, continued to be used in the field of psychopathology. In 1745, Muratori discussed the manifestation of imagination in dreams, visions, delusions and phobias, as well as in somnambulism, a condition in which marvellous feats were said to be performed. Somnambulism covered far more than sleepwalking, and included a range of phenomena that today we refer to in terms of dissociative states and altered states of consciousness. Thanks to Franz Mesmer (1734–1815), however, the discourse of imagination was displaced by a new discourse of 'animal magnetism'. Mesmer introduced to a wide public the concept of psychological healing through means that were neither directly medical (such as the use of medicine or surgery) nor theological (such as the use of exorcism to cast out evil spirits). His methods had much in common with faith healing, but he believed that his cures were mediated by an invisible fluid whose flow he was able to manipulate, and which he described in terms of metaphors rooted in the science of magnetic forces and electrical currents. Mesmer's follower, de Puységur (1751–1825) discovered how to induce a state of 'magnetic sleep', which was then thought of as 'artificial somnambulism'. 'Magnetized' individuals would closely follow the instructions of the magnetizer, disclose emotionally distressing problems and subsequently be amnesic about what had occurred. The phenomenon of post-hypnotic suggestion was described in 1787 and widely experimented with from that time on (Fancher 1979).

Mesmerism was widely practised and explored until about 1850, and in Germany in particular became a vehicle for investigating altered states of consciousness. Some individuals entered a state in which they could diagnose their own illnesses and those of others and recommend courses of treatment. In 1811, Kluge identified six levels of the magnetic state. At the fourth level, individuals manifested extrasensory perception; at the fifth, they could accurately visualize the interior of their own and others' bodies; and in the sixth, there was a 'removal of the veils of time and space and the subject perceives things hidden in the past, the future and at remote distances' (Ellenberger 1970: 78). These states fascinated those interested in paranormal phenomena and the spiritual dimensions of existence. A book written in magnetic trance by Andrew Jackson about the spirit world was to pave the way for the interest in and practical investigation of spiritualism from around 1850. In 1856, another writer explained how, in magnetic sleep, he could locate lost objects and travel through time and space. Although many leading scientists investigated these states with interest, there was inevitable conflict with the positivism upon which science and medicine were built. In due course more conservative procedures were developed, which were less likely to induce unusual states of consciousness. In Scotland, Braid learned how to induce magnetic sleep and introduced it into medicine, calling it 'hypnotism'. Other physicians performed surgery under hypnotically induced anaesthesia (the first report of this was in 1821). The theory of animal magnetism was replaced by explanations in terms of the role of suggestion in inducing changes in brain states (Ellenberger 1970; Fancher 1979).

The range of paradoxical phenomena displayed in what we now call the somatoform and dissociative disorders (American Psychiatric

Association 2000) were extensively described and discussed during the nineteenth century under the general category of 'hysteria'. The role of psychological factors was widely recognized. In 1859 Briquet identified the causes as 'violent emotions, protracted sorrows, family conflicts, and frustrated love, upon predisposed and hypersensitive persons'. In 1881 Richer identified the role of 'the patient's secret wishes' and described how a patient 'who had fallen in love with a man whom she had seen only once ... expressed in her hysterical delirium her feelings for him which she concealed in her normal state' (Ellenberger 1970: 142, 143). Detailed case studies were written of dissociative identity disorder, comparable with those reported today. In 1892, Hodgson described a case of dissociative fugue: at the age of 31, a certain Ansel Bourne briefly experienced symptoms of conversion disorder (he lost his speech, vision and hearing); much later, aged 61, he suddenly woke up disoriented, not knowing who or where he was, or why he was living in a different town under the name of Albert Brown. He had apparently been there for two months (Ellenberger 1970).

These phenomena were widely discussed in the discourse of 'animal magnetism', using terms like 'ambulatory automatism' and 'semi-somnambulism'. However, a new discourse was developing, which addressed the division of consciousness and the inconsistency of the personality. In 1890, Dessoir, in *Das Doppel-Ich* (double ego), divided the mind into an upper and a lower consciousness, the latter manifesting in dreams, hypnosis and spontaneous dissociative states. The term 'double consciousness' was used in discussing the case of Ansel Bourne above. In 1868, Durand used the term 'poly-psychism' and argued that beneath our 'ego-in-chief' lay a multi-plicity of subegos: 'each subego had a consciousness of its own, was able to perceive and to keep memories and to elaborate complex psychic operations. The sum total of these subegos constituted our unconscious life' (Ellenberger 1970: 146).

Although hypnosis remained controversial, two significant figures in France practised it, and were important influences upon Freud. Charcot (1825–93) used hypnosis to differentiate between organic conditions and the psychological conditions then called 'hysteria'. He demonstrated that conversion paralyses that occurred in response to trauma could be simulated under hypnosis. The hypnotized person could first be given the symptom and then relieved of it. Charcot did not explore the psychotherapeutic application of hypnosis because he believed that 'hysterical' symptoms and susceptibility to hypnosis had an organic basis and were due to degenerative changes in the brain. By contrast, for Bernheim (1840–1919) and the Nancy school, the key to hypnosis was suggestion. Its applications were by no means confined to 'hysteria', and they used it to treat a range of organic and psychological conditions. As Freud would also find, Bernheim realized that many positive gains could be made without hypnosis, and developed a more general approach, which, in 1891, he called 'psychotherapeutics' or 'psychotherapy' (Ellenberger 1970: 87).

Subconscious ideas and states

When William James (1891) published Volume 1 of his *Principles of Psychology* he devoted 12 pages to summarizing ten different purported 'proofs' of the existence of unconscious mental states. He dismissed each one on the same logical grounds, founded in Descartes's dualism: mental states are, by definition, conscious; an unconscious mental state is, therefore, logically impossible (James 1891: 162–75). James directly echoed Descartes: 'The first fact for us, then, as psychologists, is that thinking of some sort goes on' (1891: 224). He believed there was a soul that gave the mental realm its conscious character. However, he thought psychological theory could 'remain positivistic and non-metaphysical' (1891: 182) and could proceed without appealing to this concept, although he believed that 'things must some day be more thoroughly thought out'. He realized that mental processes were connected to brain processes and believed that 'consciousness . . . "corresponds" to the entire activity of the brain . . . at the moment' (1891: 177). However, James maintained the dualistic divide between mental processes (which are, or can be, conscious) and brain processes (which can never be conscious). He rejected the materialist position that consciousness is a mere 'epiphenomenon' of brain processes (1891: 135) and could have no causal effect, and arrived at a view similar to what is today called a 'top-down' theory (Sperry 1995), in terms of which complex conscious processes can have a causal effect on more basic physiological processes.

To support his rejection of the notion of unconscious mental states, James suggested three ways in which theorists might mistakenly conclude that there are mental states that do not give rise to conscious experience. First, in the case of aspects of perceptual processing that involve unconscious inference (as discussed above), he argued that these are not mental states at all but brain processes – 'a particular collocation of the molecules in certain tracts of the brain' (James

1891: 168). Second, he referred to the claim that unconscious processes precede the emergence into awareness of the solution of a problem; here he argued that mental states flash by so rapidly that we immediately forget about them and cannot report them. He believed that this explanation addresses another problem. When learning a skilled activity, we must, at first, pay it a lot of conscious attention. In due course, however, its runs off automatically without consciousness being directed at it. He surmised that we simply do not remember the conscious attention paid to these well learned habits, even though consciousness is still at work.

For those not convinced by these arguments, James offered yet a third argument, that conscious activity can be '*split-off* from the rest of the consciousness of the hemispheres . . . *in certain persons, the total possible consciousness may be split into parts which coexist but mutually ignore each other*' (1891: 165, 206, original italics). In such cases there is a 'primary consciousness' or 'upper consciousness', and a split off or 'secondary consciousness' or regions of consciousness that have become 'extra-marginal' or 'outside of primary consciousness'. Rather than referring to these as 'unconscious', he called them 'sub-conscious'. He did not dispute the clinical phenomena that others wrote about in terms of the language of the unconscious: he writes of 'incursions' or 'uprushes' or 'an explosion' into the 'fields of ordinary consciousness', of 'ideas' or 'energies' originating from and elaborated 'in subliminal regions of the mind' (1891: 235). When examining religious conversion, he referred to 'a conscious and voluntary way and an involuntary and unconscious way in which mental results may get accomplished' (James 1902: 206), but quickly clarified that the adjective 'unconscious', 'being a complete misnomer, is better replaced by the vaguer term "subconscious" or "subliminal"' (1902: 207). Informally, therefore, he used the term 'unconscious', but in his formal theoretical treatment he referred to 'subconscious' states because of the importance for him of the distinction between conscious states and brain processes.

Pierre Janet (1859–1947) similarly discussed certain phenomena in terms of 'subconscious', rather than 'unconscious', processes. In 1885, Janet began to study a series of patients using hypnosis. Lucie, aged 19, displayed inexplicable fits of terror. By means of automatic writing under hypnosis, she revealed that at the age of seven she had been terrified by two men who had frightened her as a practical joke. Janet attributed her terror to a 'second personality, Adrienne, who was reliving this initial episode when she had her fits of terror' (Ellenberger 1970: 358, 361). Although Janet often used the term 'unconscious' as an adjective ('unconscious personality') and as a noun ('the unconscious has its dream'), he referred to the dissociated systems (or *désagrégations*) as 'subconscious fixed ideas'. These usually originated in a 'narrowing of consciousness' precipitated by a traumatic and emotionally overwhelming event, and took the form of distorted beliefs associated with intense emotional states.

The concept is illustrated by the case of Marie (published in 1889), who experienced intense emotional distress at the time of her menstruation. Janet discovered that at menarche, feeling ashamed, she had tried to stop her menstrual flow and had eventually plunged into cold water. At each new menstruation, this fixed idea, that she must stop the menstruation, gave rise to a repetition of the symptoms. Janet realized that merely bringing the fixed idea to awareness was not enough to bring about change, and argued that the mistaken idea must be corrected. After several unsuccessful attempts to address Marie's beliefs about menstruation, he regressed her under hypnosis to the age of 13 and suggested to her that she had menstruated normally. Following this, the fixed idea appeared to have been dissolved because the symptoms dissipated. Janet did not believe that all forms of psychopathology were caused by traumatically induced subconscious fixed ideas and he went on to write widely on psychotherapy for a range of problems. However, his analysis of dissociative psychopathology is recognized today as insightful and accurate (Kihlstrom 1987).

Towards Freud

We have shown in this summary of the history of terms connected with the unconscious that over a period of two hundred years the language of unconscious mental processes or of an unconscious mind gathered momentum. These ideas were, as Whyte (1962: 63) puts it, 'conceivable around 1700, topical around 1800 and became effective around 1900'. In the same months of 1885 when Janet was starting his work with Lucie at Le Havre, Freud was visiting Charcot in Paris. As his interests rapidly turned from neurology to psychotherapy he was entering upon a fertile territory that had already begun to be widely explored. In the next chapter we see how he drew on much of the discourse presented in this chapter in making his own contribution to the concept of the unconscious, a concept that eventually came to be more associated with him than with any of those who preceded him.

C H A P T E R 3

Freud, Adler and Jung: contrasting perspectives on the psychology of the unconscious

At the start of the twentieth century, three influential figures formulated ideas about unconscious processes that profoundly influenced the field of psychotherapy in the century ahead. Yet they and their followers soon became locked in bitter power struggles. This should not surprise us. Human consciousness is very circumscribed, and any search for an understanding of unconscious factors will inevitably uncover only a small piece of the total puzzle. With the privilege of hindsight, we can see how Freud, Adler and Jung, while sharing a great deal of common ground, mapped out different areas of psychological life, so that their contributions to the understanding of unconscious processes are to a large extent complementary.

Sigmund Freud (1856–1939)

> An unconscious idea is excluded from consciousness by living forces which oppose themselves to its reception.
>
> (Freud 1912: 264)

Freud and his mentor, Josef Breuer, dismissed William James's view that the concept of unconscious ideas should be refuted on logical grounds. Breuer (1895: 223) called this mere 'juggling with words', and for Freud (1900: 612) it was a conclusion that 'the physician cannot but reject, with a shrug of his shoulders'. Freud drew on several prominent nineteenth-century ideas about unconscious processes. The first is that mental activity separates into parallel streams, only one of which can be conscious at any moment. This was referred to as 'splitting'. 'Splitting of the mind' routinely occurs when people perform activities 'mechanically' and 'with only half their mind on them' (Breuer 1895: 225–33). It also underlies the 'hysterical' phenomena observed in clinical practice. Freud (1910: 19) even referred to parallel mental activity as 'splitting of the personality'. He observed that we speak of 'the *conscious* mental state and . . . the *unconscious* one, whenever consciousness remains attached regularly to one of the two states' (original italics). The second is the idea that a sudden switching can occur from one parallel stream to another, as in cases of 'double consciousness' or the emergence of uncharacteristic behaviours. Freud (1893: 126–7) suggested that medieval nuns, who suddenly uttered 'violent blasphemies and unbridled erotic language', must have suppressed these unacceptable ideas. Rather than being annihilated, they

> enjoy an unsuspected existence in a sort of shadow kingdom, till they emerge like bad spirits and take control of the body, which is as a rule under the orders of the predominant ego-consciousness.

Breuer referred to such phenomena as 'splitting . . . of consciousness'.

The third idea is that one aspect of mental activity renders another 'inadmissible to consciousness' (Breuer 1895: 222). Using several terms interchangeably, Freud refers to 'inhibition', 'suppression' (1893: 127), 'fending off' (1895b: 157) an idea, 'decid[ing] to forget about it . . . pushing the thing away . . . not thinking about it' (1894: 47). In the case of Lucy R, there was a 'deliberate and intentional' act of 'repudiation' as a result of which an 'incompatible idea' was 'repressed into the unconscious' and 'isolate[d] psychically' (Freud 1895a: 122–3). Of all these terms, it was 'repression' that Freud mainly used in his theoretical expositions. The fourth idea was that conscious activity is influenced by the unconscious. Freud (1910: 19) observed that post-hypnotic suggestion, in which 'a command given under hypnosis is slavishly carried out subsequently in the normal state', provided 'an admirable example of the influences which the unconscious state can exercise over the conscious one'. Breuer expressed what Freud (1912: 261) would come to call the 'dynamic view' of the unconscious:

> part of the mind [is] thrust into darkness [a quotation from Goethe's Faust] as the Titans are imprisoned in the crater of Etna. [From there they] can shake the earth but can never emerge into the light of day . . . unconscious ideas govern the . . . [patient's]

inexplicable, unreasonable changes of feeling ... the 'split-off mind' acts like a sounding-board to the note of a tuning fork. Any event that provokes unconscious memories liberates the whole affective force of these ideas ... [which] is then quite out of proportion to any that would have arisen in the conscious mind alone.

(Breuer 1895: 229, 237)

Finally, there is the metaphor of depth. Freud (1895c: 300) refers to 'ideas which are derived from the greatest depth', and writes of how, by approaching 'the material in the deeper layers' he hoped to 'discover ... the connecting threads' (1895c: 293). Eugene Bleuler would use this metaphor when he coined the phrase 'depth psychology' to refer to Freud's psychoanalytic approach (Freud 1914: 41). In discussing the psychotherapy of Elizabeth von R, Freud used the more specific metaphor of 'excavating a buried city'; this involved 'clearing away the pathogenic psychical material layer by layer' (Freud 1895b: 139). There is a similar connotation of clearing away, but less one of depth in the metaphor of 'chimney sweeping', used by Breuer's patient Anna O to refer to her recovery of traumatic memories and her expression of the associated emotions.

Defence and repression and their consequences

Against this background, Freud carefully examined specific psychological processes and documented them in detailed case studies. He recognized that individuals were often aware of the source of their emotional distress even if they could not easily disclose it to others; once they could confess to a priest or confide in a friend, they would feel relief and any symptoms would resolve. Freud (1895c: 286) called this 'retention'. He contrasted this with 'defence', where the process of repression was out of awareness and occurred so automatically that individuals were unaware of the source of their symptoms. As Freud focused more and more on defence, he was already doubtful about whether there were cases of (consciously controlled) retention in which there was not also an unconscious defensive component.

This led to his elaboration of the dynamic view of the unconscious. Repressed material was the source of an 'unconscious intelligence' (Freud 1895c: 275) whose influence could be detected in a variety of situations. In the process of 'conversion' the emotional charge associated with repressed material could be 'transformed into something somatic' (Freud 1894: 49). For example, Elizabeth von R's repressed love for her sister's husband gave rise to persistent pains and weakness in her legs, while it lay 'concealed, all that time, behind the mask of mere sisterly affection' (Freud 1895b: 158). The unconscious made its presence felt not only in clinical symptoms but in everyday slips of the tongue and the 'motivated forgetting' of words with uncomfortable associations (Freud 1901; see also Example 2 on p. 3). Furthermore, 'we are probably inclined greatly to over-estimate the conscious character of intellectual and artistic production' (Freud 1900: 613). Jokes too could be understood as indirect allusions to repressed material (Freud 1905).

Freud offered a detailed theory of the relationship between conscious and unconscious activity in dreams, which, above all, he saw as *'the royal road to a knowledge of the unconscious activities of the mind'* (Freud 1900: 608, original italics). He gave many examples from his own self-analysis. In the 1890s, he suffered somatic symptoms, depressed moods, unreasonable jealousy and intense hatred (Gay 1989). He undertook his own free association exercises, seeking to recover childhood memories. He recalled, for example, an overnight railway journey, when he was four, on which, as he put it, his 'libido toward *matrem* had awakened' when he had the opportunity to 'see her *nudam*'. As Gay (1989: 11) observes, even Freud, the great unveiler of secrets, veiled in Latin terms the discovery of his repressed erotic feelings for his mother on seeing her naked. His self-analysis enabled him to document from his own experience the influence of repressed memories on the content of a dream. Memories of distressing events were too painful to be admitted to consciousness, he claimed, and were subjected to a process of censorship and disguise by the mechanisms of 'dream work', which included the representation of familiar things or people in symbolic form. The series of confusing and bizarre scenes and images, which often made reference to events from the day before ('day's residues'), constituted the dream's 'manifest content'. However, the key to the meaning of the dream lay in the unconscious influences of repressed material, which constituted the 'latent content'.

Four views of the unconscious

In 1915, Freud systematically summarized his theories and presented four different 'views' of the unconscious. First, from the 'descriptive' perspective, most psychological activity is unconscious, in the sense of being out of immediate awareness. Taking a position remarkably close to the contemporary theory of Baars (1997), Freud (1915b: 171) likened the perception of mental processes 'by means of consciousness to the perception of the external world by the sense organs'. Just as our senses pick up only a small part of what is there in the external world, so consciousness attends to only a small part of available mental activity. The second or 'dynamic view', already discussed above, focuses on the influence of repressed material on consciousness. Freud now distinguished between *'primal repression'*, which happened when instinctual material was so threatening that it never passed the threshold of consciousness at all, and *'repression proper'* (Freud 1915a: 148, original italics), which referred to the exclusion of material that had been in full awareness. Repression was now understood to be the main mechanism of defence.

According to the third, 'topographical' (Freud 1915b: 172), view, there are three interacting systems, a conscious 'system *Cs*', a descriptively unconscious 'system *Pcs*' ('preconscious') and a repressed unconscious 'system *Ucs*'. The system *Cs* exercised censorship over the system *Ucs* and prevented threatening material from becoming conscious; there was some milder form of censorship between the *Cs* and the *Pcs*. The fourth 'economic' view conceptualized the way in which 'excitation' was activated, transformed and transmitted within and between these systems. The 'cathexis' (excitation) of repressed 'libido' or sexual excitation could be converted into somatic symptoms, but it could also be discharged as anxiety 'without the subject knowing what he is afraid of', or displaced to other 'psychical activity', such as phobias and obsessional ruminations (1915b: 181, 182). He distinguished between the orderly and rational 'secondary process' thinking of the system *Pcs/Cs*, and the chaotic and irrational 'primary process' of the system *Ucs*. 'The nucleus of the *Ucs* . . . consists of wishful impulses', wrote Freud (1915b: 186); that is, instinctual impulses that seek expression. Related to these are 'ideas' (memories and images) that express the impulse. These exist side by side without any structure, but they may be more or less 'cathected' at any moment. Two completely incompatible ideas might be cathected simultaneously (the principle of 'exemption from mutual contradiction'); the ideas are 'timeless (i.e. they are not ordered temporally, they are not altered by the passage of time)' (1915b: 187); nor are they subject to reality testing. Two features which he had identified as central to dreams were most characteristic of primary process: displacement, in which the cathexis activating one idea could simply transfer itself to another completely different one; and condensation, where the cathexis of several ideas might be joined in a single image.

The primary process of the *Ucs* is largely unnoticed because of the 'reality principle' (Freud 1920: 10): instinctual impulses, which are governed by the 'pleasure principle', must pass through the *Pcs* and therefore be subjected to secondary process organization before they can control behaviour. Language in particular, with its rules of logic and its capacity to order material coherently, plays a central role in secondary process thinking. If a repressed impulse or image passes fleetingly into consciousness (for example, during free association) it will not remain in the system *Cs* unless words are found for it. To emerge fully into consciousness, therefore, material needs to be put into words (see Chapter 8 for a fuller examination of this point).

Id, ego, superego and beyond

Critics of Freud's theory of the unconscious usually focus on his topographical and economic models. However, Freud himself realized the limitations of the topographical model, which conflated the content of awareness with the ego that controlled behaviour. It was a Cartesian heroic consciousness, rational, insightful and actively checking out material in the *Ucs* that must be kept repressed. Freud (1901) used the metaphor of a doorkeeper who carefully selects, from people crowded in an antechamber, whom he will admit to the chamber of consciousness. Critics such as Sartre and Boss (see Chapter 4) pointed out that this was self-contradictory. How could the doorkeeper be conscious of material that was unconscious? Freud's answer to this emerged from observations of the ways clients resisted engaging in the work of psychotherapy. Behind resistance lay defensive processes that he had long recognized were 'unconscious' (Freud 1896: 162) though not repressed. Furthermore, repression was only one of several mechanisms of defence. His new structural model was designed to accommodate this (Freud 1920, 1923a). He used the term 'id' for the domain of instincts and wishes, much though not all of which was repressed and unconscious. The 'coherent ego' referred to those structured processes which accommodate behaviour to the demands of physical and social reality; these included the processes of defence and 'the motives of the resistances, and indeed the resistances themselves, [which] are unconscious at first'. This meant that 'much of the ego is itself unconscious; only a small part of it is covered by the term 'preconscious' (Freud 1920: 19). The doorkeeper, therefore, represented an unconscious aspect of the ego. This reformulation accompanied a major shift in psychotherapy technique from the analysis of repressed material to the analysis of resistance and defence. Much later, Freud (1940) also observed the lack of coherence in the ego itself. It could split into different modes, which would manifest themselves at different times in response to the requirements of defence.

However, not all resistance came from the ego. An 'unconscious sense of guilt' (Freud 1923a: 27) furnished a different kind of resistance, located in another structure, the 'superego'. This 'precipitate in the ego' carried identification with the values of the parents and contained internalized precepts such as 'You *ought to be* like this (like your father)' and prohibitions like 'You *may not be* like this (like your father)' (Freud 1923a: 34, original italics). Aspects of the superego were therefore unconscious. Another source of resistance was the compulsion to engage repetitively in neurotic behaviour patterns (Freud 1920). On the positive side, this repetition suggested a drive to address (unconsciously) the source of neurotic behaviour. In practice, however, it interfered with getting to the root of the problem. He referred to this resistance, which did not come from the ego or the superego, as 'the *resistance of the unconscious*' (Freud 1926: 160, original italics).

These theoretical formulations reveal one side of Freud, the former neurologist who was interested in rigorously structured scientific theories. Those who came into conflict with him found this side of him dogmatic and inflexible. Yet Freud was aware of the danger of rigid theorizing and often quoted Charcot, who had remarked: 'theory is all very well, but that does not prevent facts from existing' (Gay 1989: 51). In discussing his structural model, he warns of the danger of 'taking abstractions too rigidly'. Often, he observes, we can say that 'the ego is identical with the id, and is merely a differentiated part of it'. Similarly, for many purposes, ego and superego 'are merged . . . we can only distinguish one from another when there is a tension of conflict between them' (Freud 1926: 97). This points to another side of Freud – Freud the inheritor of the literary and romantic traditions of European culture. He had been impressed by the antique statues he saw in the Louvre, on his first visit to Paris, and later acquired a collection of his own (Gay 1989). He was absorbed in mythological and literary themes and regularly spoke of how 'the great poets and writers had preceded psychologists in the exploration of the human mind' (Ellenberger 1970: 467). He keenly followed archaeological discoveries, and wrote a short piece (Freud 1911) on the veneration at Ephesus of the goddess Diana in ancient times, on its continuation with the veneration of Mary during Christian times and on the recent dream of a German girl in which Diana had appeared and directed her to a house in the ruins of Ephesus, a house that was found and became an object of pilgrimage. He wrote to Alfons Paquet, who had informed him that he had been awarded the Goethe Prize, that 'I have never before found the secret, personal intentions behind [my work] recognized with such clarity as by you' (Freud 1930: 207). This side of Freud recognized the role of symbols in dreams, and accepted that, while the meaning of many dream symbols was fairly self-evident, others were more obscure and could not simply be explained from the common language that individuals share. As we shall see, some of his more expansive ideas are surprisingly close to those of Jung.

Alfred Adler (1870–1937)

> To prevent its being unmasked, the *feeling of inferiority* ... [creates] a compensatory psychic suprastructure [which] seeks to regain, by means of fully tested preparations and defences, a point of vantage and superiority in life.
>
> (Adler 1913a: 32, original italics)

> It is only the individual-psychological method that can then throw light upon these phenomena of the unconscious and that can attempt to correct a false development.
>
> (Adler 1912a: 22)

In his career as a physician, Adler was concerned about the role of social upliftment and education in the prevention of diseases. He sought to improve the quality of life in society at large by developing *Menschenkenntnis*, practical knowledge of human nature, which could serve as a basis for programmes of education and training (Ellenberger 1970). He brought these values and perspectives to the field of mental health, when he began to practice psychotherapy, probably in his late twenties; and by the time he became a founding member of Freud's psychoanalytic circle in 1902, the central features of his approach were already established.

For Adler the root of psychological problems lay in the way in which children learned to compensate, in a variety of ways, for an underlying sense of inferiority. He was familiar with the role of compensation from his experiences as a physician. It was widely known that, where children had a defective physical organ, the body would make compensatory adjustments to enable the child to function and survive. Adler recognized that there were also processes of psychological compensation. Children suffering from 'organ inferiority' (Adler 1911: 80) usually experienced a corresponding psychological inferiority in comparison to peers, and mechanisms of psychological compensation came into play, which helped the child to cope with the situation. A sense of insecurity or inferiority could also arise from the emotional climate in which children were raised; being deprived or mistreated could cause it, but so too could being spoiled and pampered, since this undermines the child's capacity to cope with the demands of life.

For example, 'a sickly girl' who feels chronically insecure 'strives to became superior to her mother . . . [and] leans on her father . . . as if she were his wife' (Adler 1912b: x). This compensatory role provides her with a 'heightened ego-consciousness' and an accompanying sense of security and stability. Furthermore, 'misinterpretations made in early childhood' (Adler 1930; Ansbacher and Ansbacher 1958: 183) and the compensatory structures put in place to deal with them are usually carried into adult life. Much can be understood about individual personalities in terms of the diverse ways in which people actively distance from and compensate for underlying inferiority feelings. Although it was not confined to men, Adler (1912a: 49) initially called this compensatory activity the 'masculine protest'. This was 'a choice of metaphor which was not a particularly happy one' (Ansbacher and Ansbacher 1958: 45), but in the gendered discourse of the time it was a natural step to describe a part of the self that is experienced as weak or ineffectual as 'feminine' or 'effeminate', and to use a phrase like 'masculine protest' (Adler 1913a: 34) for psychological processes that work against that part. Later, this term was largely replaced by the term 'striving for superiority' because the goal of the compensatory strategies was to cover the underlying inferiority with a sense of dominance over others.

When we look closely at neurotic behaviour, Adler argues, we find individuals who are 'struggling for recognition, actually attempting to force it; . . . aspiring ceaselessly to a godlike dominance over the environment from out the region of [their] insecurity and the sense of inferiority'. They achieve this by means of a 'compensatory psychic superstructure' (Adler 1913a: 31–2), which incorporates an elaborate 'system of protective safeguards' (Stepansky 1983: 119). Adler called this system a 'guiding fiction'. It is a 'fiction' because it is entirely of the individual's own construction. It is 'guiding' because it serves to organize the characteristic mode of functioning that permeates people's response to every situation, their *'neurotic modus vivendi'* (Adler 1913a: 32), their 'method of facing problems' or their 'style of life' (Adler 1932: 212). The girl referred to above, for example, consistently takes refuge in her father and will not do anything that might threaten her ties to him: when she grows up she may refuse offers of marriage. Some might use depression and social withdrawal to avoid the kinds of situations that might evoke the underlying inferiority feelings. Some bolster their superiority by deprecatory attacks on others. However, since behaving in an aggressive and disdainful manner can result in being discredited as envious, greedy and hostile, some individuals construct a socially acceptable 'anti-fiction' that presents themselves as pleasant and friendly. They contrive to bolster self-esteem while appearing to be modest and humble, 'to shine through modesty, to conquer by humility and submissiveness, to humiliate others by one's virtues, to attack others by one's own passivity' (Adler 1912b: 40–3). They also develop a heightened vigilance to the probable consequences of their behaviour moment to moment. They 'pay attention to relationships which still escape others', become exaggeratedly cautious and begin 'to anticipate all sorts of disagreeable consequences in starting out to do something'. It is as if they have special 'antennae [which] test all the phenomena of the environment and examine them constantly for their advantages and disadvantages with regard to the assumed goal', which is to 'exclud[e] from experience every permanent degradation' (1912b: xii–xv).

Adler used various metaphors to point to how individuals are unaware of their role in setting up these processes or in maintaining them in the present. 'There is nothing that sets to work with greater secrecy than the construction of the ideal of personality,' he wrote. Since the guiding fiction is selfishly motivated and antisocial it 'must early become unrecognizable, must assume a disguise, or it destroys itself'. As a result, people fail to recognize the 'circuitous ways comparable to secret paths' that are the source of their unhappiness, despite the fact that they are of their own construction. Adler also used the language of the unconscious. The guiding fictions 'act secretly within the unconscious' and are so influential that 'unconsciously [the neurotic] has become incapable of proceeding freely and without prejudice to the solution of real problems' (Adler 1912b: 9, 40, 43). Similarly, defiant behaviour in children is based on unconscious erroneous attitudes ... The starting point, the erroneous attitude, and the final goal of the masculine protest are withdrawn from consciousness, and the whole sequence of effects necessarily takes place in the unconscious.

(Adler 1910 in Ansbacher and Ansbacher 1958: 55)

Adler's is a constructivist theory within which individual behaviour and experience is founded on personal meaning. Drawing on the nineteenth-century concept of apperception (see Chapter 2), Adler observes how children develop their own 'schema of apperception', the organized structure of meanings that embodies 'the opinion which the child ... has gained of himself and the world' (Adler 1930 in Ansbacher and Ansbacher 1958: 182). Vaihinger, whom Adler greatly admired, reformulated this approach in 1911 and observed that cognitive functioning occurs

for the most part unconsciously. Should the product finally enter consciousness also, this light only penetrates to the shallows, and the actual fundamental processes are carried on in the darkness of the unconscious.

(Ansbacher and Ansbacher 1958: 78)

But this was not the unconscious as Freud saw it, at least not in the first decade of the century. His theories were founded on a biological model, within which instinctual drives were repressed by socialized consciousness. This clash between Freud's biologism and Adler's constructivism led to the intense debates in the Vienna Psychoanalytic Society that ended in Adler's resignation in 1911. Adler believed that Freud exaggerated the importance of biological factors and instinctual drives. Many of the problem behaviours with which psychotherapy deals appear childish, he argued, not because they are expressions of repressed instincts, but because they are habits formed in childhood which have never lost their childish character. What Freud saw as the products of repressed libido, Adler saw as consequences of the guiding fiction, designed to protect the individual from inferiority feelings. Freud saw Adler's position as a complete rejection of the dynamic view of the unconscious. It was no more than

ego psychology deepened by knowledge of the psychology of the unconscious ... Adler has tried to bring us, who gathered together to investigate the vicissitudes of the libido, nearer to surface psychology.

(Colby 1958: 71, 73)

There was also discourse politics at work. Freud wanted Adler's insights to be assimilated into his own language: the underlying insecurities sounded like the system *Ucs*; Adler's ego-consciousness sounded like the system *Cs/Pcs*; and the masculine protest seemed like a synonym for repression and defence. Freud observed:

I take it ill . . . that [Adler] speaks of the same things without designating them by the same names which they already have and without trying to bring his new terms into relationship with the old.

(Colby 1958: 70)

A few years later, Janet would make a similar complaint about Freud:

what I had called psychological analysis, he called psycho-analysis; what I had called a psychological system . . . he called a complex; he considered a repression what I considered a restriction of consciousness.

(Janet 1924: 41)

Each theorist is attracted by specific terms and metaphors, which gain their meaning partly from personal associations and partly from habit. It is always far more comfortable to have other people use one's own construct system than to have to accommodate oneself to another person's construct system, with which one is likely to feel less congruent.

Adler's model was founded on the principle of cognitive consistency and did not portray conscious and unconscious as fundamentally different from or in opposition to each other. Instead, what is conscious or unconscious is arranged according to the purposes of the guiding fiction: 'Consciousness and unconsciousness move together in the same direction and are not contradictions, as is often believed. What is more, there is no definite line of demarcation between them' (Adler 1930: 56). Any antithesis 'is only an antithesis of means' (Adler 1913b: 229); material is kept unconscious in the interests of cognitive consistency, since inconsistency threatens the protective superstructure. Consciousness is, therefore, 'merely a device of the psyche' for ensuring self-consistency: 'when . . . the neurotic goal might nullify itself by coming into direct opposition with the feeling of the community [i.e. with consciously held attitudes and values] then its life plan is formed in the unconscious'. However, 'even the fictive goal, even the neurotic life-plan can partially become conscious' where this supports an enhancement of self-esteem and does not threaten 'the unity of the personality' (i.e. cognitive consistency) (1913b: 229–30).

Thus the task of psychotherapy is not the uncovering of repressed impulses, but the bringing to consciousness of the inconsistencies inherent in the 'guiding idea of greatness' (1913b: 230) and the 'devices and arrangements' (Adler 1913a: 31) that support it. Adler set out to catalyse change, by provoking what we now call cognitive dissonance. He described discussions with an 11-year-old girl who would, on every morning of a school day, become extremely anxious and demanding. He gently introduced various ideas, such as how it is normal for spoiled only children to learn that they can get attention in this way. In due course, he observed, she will awaken one morning 'with the realization: "I am about to stir up a commotion in my family." And being aware of it, she can then avoid it' (Adler 1930; Ansbacher and Ansbacher 1958: 398). This approach has been compared to that of Socrates: 'Adler had all Socrates' irony, his teasing slyness, his art of luring patients into the dialectical traps of self-contradiction . . . his treatment of patients bore a strong likeness to the Socratic method of conducting an argument' (Way 1950: 305).

Like Freud, Adler refers to repression:

> [when] the feeling of inferiority finds expression in the fear of the sexual partner . . . [t]he fiction may . . . repress the incentive to perversion into the subconscious or make the fear of the partner unrecognizable to consciousness.
>
> (Adler 1912b: 32)
> [*Note Adler's use of 'subconscious', interchangeable with 'unconscious', something we find occasionally in Jung (e.g. 1902: 73) too.*]

However, for Adler repression was not a physical metaphor implying the damming up of libido. Rather than being the key to neurotic behaviour, it was just one of many safeguarding tendencies that protected the consistency of the consciously held view of self and reality, by relegating inconsistent material to the unconscious.

Freud's structural model eventually incorporated many of the features of Adler's theory. Adler (1938: 202), who was deliberately increasing the distinctiveness of his own discourse by moving away from the language of 'the unconscious', observed somewhat mockingly: 'even the so-called conscious, or ego, is chock full of the unconscious, or as I have called it, the not-understood'. Terms like 'not-understood' and 'hidden' were the alternative discourse with which he replaced the term 'unconscious'. This shift was not merely politically motivated, but was based on an additional insight: that a great deal of the organization that underlies the style of life is out of awareness, having formed at a time when the child 'has neither language nor ideas adequate to give it expression'. Its further development 'has never been comprehended in words and is therefore not open to the assaults of criticism'. As a result, 'there can be no question here of anything like a repressed unconscious; it is rather a question of something not understood; of something withheld from the understanding' (Adler 1938: 16).

Carl Gustav Jung (1875–1961)

> Without history, there can be no psychology, and certainly no psychology of the unconscious.
>
> (Jung 1977: 232)

> Consciousness . . . must always remain the smaller circle within the greater circle of the unconscious, an island surrounding itself with the sea; and, like the sea itself, the unconscious yields an endless and self-replenishing abundance of living creatures, a wealth beyond our fathoming.
>
> (Jung 1946: 177)

This second quotation at once reveals Jung's appreciation of Freud and his marked differences. Freud (1900: 612) himself had written, 'The unconscious is the larger sphere which includes within it the smaller sphere of the conscious', but what Jung meant by an 'abundance of living creatures' went far beyond anything that Freud could admit. Unusual experiences, even as a child, introduced him to the complexity of the human psyche and the dialectical relationship between conscious and unconscious processes. He would later observe that his 'intellectual life had its unconscious beginnings' at the age of four, in a dream of a 'subterranean god' in the form of a ritual phallus, a dream that 'was to preoccupy me all my life' (Jung 1977: 26–30). Aged six, he was deeply interested in the rich illustrations in a book of Hindu mythology, and was fascinated by the museum in Basel. A few years later, he suddenly felt a deep nostalgia as an old-fashioned carriage passed by, and thought, 'that comes from *my* times . . . Yes, that's how it was!' (1977: 50). In a talk he gave in 1896, entitled 'On the limits of the exact sciences', he attacked materialism and advocated the study of spiritism and hypnosis (Ellenberger 1970). All this prefigured the subsequent development of his theories.

In his dissertation, Jung reviewed the classic cases of 'somnambulism', 'semisomnambulism', 'automatism' and 'double consciousness'. He was fascinated by the way in which complex activities are subtly controlled by processes 'whose results are not available for the conscious psychic activity of the individual'. He found an example of cryptamnesia in Nietzsche's *Also sprach Zarathustra*: a ship's crew go ashore to shoot rabbits and see Zarathustra, flying through the air and into the mouth of a volcano. Nietzsche's sister told Jung that, as a teenager, Nietzsche had read a book that described some seamen going ashore to shoot rabbits and seeing two men flying through the air and into the crater of Mount Stromboli. This forgotten memory 'must have slipped half or wholly unconsciously into his mind' when Nietzsche wrote this passage, suggests Jung (1902: 80–3). He saw similar subtle processes at work at a series of seances at which his cousin, Helene, went into trance. He noted how a participant may 'assume unconscious control of the table movements' (1902: 49) by initiating little taps or tremors, and how Helene exhibited 'heightened unconscious performance' (1902: 80), speaking fluently in a different dialect of German, as she personified several deceased family members, including her (and Jung's) grandfather.

Jung's 'collision with the unconscious'

Jung conducted a series of studies of word association. Ziehen had shown that longer reaction times to specific words pointed to emotionally charged underlying material, which he called a 'feeling-toned complex'. This behaves like 'a quasi-independent entity – a "second consciousness"' (Jung 1905: 262), but usually lies hidden 'in the depths of the mind' and exerts its effect 'unconsciously', so that participants are unaware of the emotional significance of the delayed reaction time. We 'unconsciously take an item from our memories', Jung (1906: 419, 424) observed, and 'our reactions . . . are determined to the smallest detail by our complexes'. This converged with Freud's formulations; in 1906, Jung began an enthusiastic correspondence with him; and in 1910 became founding president of the International Psychoanalytic Association. However, differences from Freud were apparent from the start, and, like Adler, he never used the language of the 'system *Cs*' and the 'system *Ucs*'. Furthermore, Jung began to envisage a stage of therapy that went beyond what Freud and Adler offered. This was a development of his long-standing sense of history, which now rose up to meet him even more forcefully in his dreams. In 1909, on a voyage to Massachusetts, Freud, Jung and Ferenczi shared and analysed their dreams. Jung dreamed he owned a house with several storeys. Upstairs was a comfortable room with fine furniture in rococo style. The ground floor was dark, with brick floors and medieval furniture, as if from the fifteenth or sixteenth century. Below was a cellar with Roman architecture, and, below this, a cave in which were pieces of broken pottery and 'two human skulls, obviously very old and half disintegrated' (Jung 1977: 182). Freud focused on these skulls and asked Jung whether there were two individuals whom he wished dead. Jung, for whom the dream pointed to the broader historical matrix within which individual life is embedded, found Freud's approach limiting, but could find no way to offer Freud 'any insight into my mental world . . . he was completely helpless in dealing with certain kinds of dreams' (1977: 183). Another dream, in 1912, was of a row of tombs in a church vault that spanned some 800 years. Effigies of the dead lay 'in their antique clothes, not hewn out of stone, but in a curious fashion mummified' (1977: 196). Each one slowly came to life as Jung walked past. As Jung's understanding evolved to encompass dreams like these, his divergences from Freud intensified. In 1914 he resigned from the International Psychoanalytic Association and broke with Freud completely.

These dreams ushered in a psychological crisis. Between 1913 and 1919, Jung experienced a 'collision with the unconscious' (Jung 1942: 32). He lived 'as if under constant inner pressure . . . one thunderstorm followed another', as he endured a series of 'assaults of the unconscious'. He found relief in playing for hours at the edge of the lake, building a village out of stones. This evoked deep numinous feelings, and a flood of imagery, which expressed intense and otherwise obscure feelings and provided meaning and reassurance:

> Had I left these images hidden in the emotions I might have been torn to pieces by them . . . I learned how helpful it can be . . . to find the particular images which lie behind emotions.
>
> (Jung 1977: 197, 201)

He would also draw or paint the images or let them unfold in the process he called 'active imagination' (Jung 1958b: 68).

Persona, shadow and the archetypes of the collective unconscious

These psychological forces, pointing beyond the details of personal biography, led Jung to develop a historical perspective on the relationship between conscious and unconscious. Human consciousness was but 'a late-born descendent of the unconscious psyche' (Jung 1931a: 350), which had evolved in response to the development of 'civilized life', with its demand for 'concentrated, directed, conscious functioning' (Jung 1958b: 71), for an internally consistent view of things and the need to mould oneself into 'an ideal image' (Jung 1934: 155). One effect of this is that life easily becomes unbalanced, and the unconscious plays an important role in 'compensating the one-sidedness of consciousness' (Jung 1958b: 73), providing the opportunity to restore the balance. The unconscious had a personal layer, as Freud had recognized, but beyond this was a 'deeper layer of the unconscious where the primordial images common to humanity lie sleeping' (Jung 1942: 64), and from where images of ancient times could spontaneously arise. This was 'the collective unconscious' – he also called it 'an impersonal or transpersonal unconscious' – the site of 'ancient thought-forms . . . as much feelings as thoughts', which were 'deposits of the constantly repeated experiences of humanity' (Jung 1958b: 68), which had 'taken aeons to form' (Jung 1948: 93) and which are the inheritance of all, whatever their race or culture. This was more than a memory bank; it was a separate reality with its own autonomous existence, 'an internal spiritual world whose existence we never suspected' (Jung 1942: 76). Within it could be found 'living entities which exert an attractive force upon the conscious mind' (Jung 1934: 142). These 'archetypes' or 'dominants' were powerful spiritual forces with 'their own independent life' (Jung 1942: 65). 'There is some justification', he observed, 'for the old view of the soul as an objective reality' (Jung 1931a: 347).

Jung's discourse drew heavily on metaphor. What people present publicly is a mask – he used the word 'persona', the mask worn by actors in ancient Greek theatre. This creates an illusion of individuality: when 'we strip off the mask' we discover 'the essential individuality of the person', compared to which the persona is no more than 'a secondary reality'. For what the mask conceals, he used another metaphor – of a shadow, where lie 'those contents that refuse to fit into the whole [and which] are either overlooked ... or repressed' (Jung 1934: 155–6). As Jung draws on different aspects of the metaphor, the shadow shifts in meaning. What lies in the shadows is likely to go unnoticed; my own shadow may be more apparent to others than to myself; however hard I try, I cannot get away from my shadow, it inevitably follows me. 'The essential thing is not the shadow but the body that casts it' (Jung 1930: 64), he observes, criticizing Freud for focusing excessively on uncovering repressed material. Furthermore, individuals do not see what lies in their shadow as belonging to themselves, but see it projected on to others (projection is discussed by Grant and Crawley 2002). Those who have disowned their anger see others as angry; those who have disowned their eroticism see others as obsessed with sex. Since it is 'the unconscious which does the projecting', Jung (1950: 9) observed, it is not easy to convince a person that he or she 'casts a very long shadow'.

At first in facing the shadow one is dealing with 'the personal unconscious (which corresponds to Freud's conception of the unconscious)' (Jung 1939: 284). However, one quickly apprehends that one is dealing with more than repressed personal material; one is entering the shadows cast by the culture at large, and by the unfolding of history. The shadow is therefore also an archetypal aspect of the collective unconscious. Jung encountered this in a dream in which he and a dark-skinned 'savage' killed the German warrior hero Siegfried. He was overcome by grief and guilt. Upon reflection he realized that at a personal level Siegfried represented a ruthless will to power, which 'no longer suited me' (Jung 1977: 205). He dreamed this in 1913 at a time when he sensed that Europe was moving inexorably towards a catastrophic confrontation. Siegfried also represented the archetypal forces that lay behind the rising German nationalism. At a collective level, the dark-skinned man points to the possibility of a simpler, more authentic existence, which had been obscured within the European culture and way of life.

Confronting the shadow is the first stage of a spiritual journey that Jung called 'individuation'. The process is set in motion by the 'self archetype', an 'unconscious self', which acts like a guiding force towards the discovery of one's own 'authentic being', one's 'real self', the source of one's 'own real potentialities' (Jung 1934: 158). Even more mysterious forces now present themselves, often in the form of images from mythology or ancient history. Individuals might find themselves immersed in 'the whole symbolism of initiation ... clear and unmistakable' (1934: 228), as if engaged in the kind of rites of passage described in the religious and shamanic traditions. The next step in the transformation process is integration of the spiritual qualities of the opposite sex. This involves encounters with numinous archetypal presences: for men this is the anima, who appears as mythic princesses or queens, or goddesses; for women, it is the animus, who appears as mythic kings or princes, or gods. The classic symbol of the sacred marriage portrays the completion of this process. This is just one of many parallels Jung found in the medieval texts on alchemy, in the ancient scriptures of the Gnostics and in the spiritual classics of the world's great religions. He concluded that such images are 'projection[s] of the collective unconscious' (Jung 1931b: 152). 'Mythological ideas', he remarked, 'with their extraordinary symbolism evidently reach far into the human psyche and touch the historical foundations where reason, will and good intentions never penetrate' (Jung 1935: 15). They offer the basis for further evolution, not only for each individual, but for the culture as a whole. The human race has not yet 'attained the highest possible degree of consciousness . . . There must be some potential unconscious psyche left over whose development would result in . . . a higher differentiation of consciousness' (Jung 1946: 190).

'My life', Jung (1977: 17) observed, 'is a story of the self-realization of the unconscious.' He felt he had no choice about this; it was as if he was 'obeying a higher will' (1977: 201). But individuation calls for 'a willingness to undergo a complete transformation of the human being' (Wehr 1987: 164) and is not something to be undertaken lightly. Jung (1946: 186) likened it to 'a surgical operation' which is resorted to 'only . . . when other methods have failed'. A great deal of attention needs to be paid, therefore, to finding a way to sustain a 'running conversation with the unconscious' (Jung 1942: 109). Although guidelines can be given, he warned, no programme can be offered 'in the form of a recipe' (Jung 1939: 289). He himself managed it by living with careful discipline, keeping himself grounded in the tasks and realities of home and therapy practice, and devoting time to reflection on and intellectual understanding of the emerging material. At first the unconscious must be allowed to take the lead as the individual works to experience the feelings and let them take form in imagery, dancing, drawing, painting or sculpture. However, since the unconscious does not work to 'a deliberate and concerted plan and is [not] striving to realize certain definite ends' (Jung 1934: 182), it cannot be relied on to direct the process entirely. The conscious or ego must take the lead in sustaining an active dialogue between conscious and unconscious, which must stand side by side as equal partners in the process. If this is successful, the process unfolds until the seeming opposites are united and there is 'a living birth that leads to a new level of being' (Jung 1958b: 90).

Synchronicity and psychic infection

Jung's perspective was more like that of a shamanic healer than a medical scientist. He had undergone a 'creative illness' from which he emerged with a profoundly changed understanding and 'an increased propensity to intuitions, psychical experiences and meaningful dreams' (Ellenberger 1970: 673). Paranormal phenomena such as telepathy and clairvoyance became routine features of his life, and he conceptualized them in terms of 'synchronicity' (Jung 1958a), a principle whereby apparently separate external events might be connected through an underlying meaningful connection in the timeless world of archetypes. This transpersonal approach provided a unique perspective on phenomena associated with what Freud had called transference (see Grant and Crawley 2002). In transference, clients form with their therapist 'a bond that corresponds in every respect to the initial infantile relationship, with a tendency to recapitulate all the experiences of childhood on the doctor' (Jung 1946: 170). This is often associated with a disturbing impact that the client seems unconsciously to exert on the therapist, an 'almost "chemical" action' (Jung 1930: 72). Jung saw this as being mediated by 'an activated unconscious content' in the client being transferred to the therapist by a process of 'unconscious infection'. Such 'psychic infections' (Jung 1946: 175, 176) are an inevitable feature of a therapist's work and all therapists must learn how to deal with them; we return to contemporary perspectives on this in Chapter 7 (pp. 106–11).

Jung recognized that his was not a theory that addressed most people's everyday experience; direct experience of the collective unconscious and the archetypes was 'unknown to most people and . . . bound to seem strange' (Jung 1934: 238). It certainly was to the practical mind of Adler, who had no time for the paranormal. Freud too largely steered clear of it. Jung refers to Freud's 'notoriously negative attitude to the psychic reality of archetypal images' and criticized him for 'fail[ing] to do justice to the obvious admixture of archetypal data' (Freud 1946: 185). However, we have seen that Freud had another side to him. His interest in 'unconscious phantasies', vivid images and scenes with a memory-like quality that emerge during the course of psychotherapy led him to express views which converged with Jung's. These images seem to have their origins in 'the childhood of humanity' (Gay 1989: 368), wrote Freud in 1915, and 'to be a fragment of extremely ancient inherited mental equipment' (Freud 1923b: 242). In the last year of his life, Freud (1939: 99–100) stated the controversial conclusion that 'the archaic heritage of human beings comprises not only dispositions but also subject matter – memory-traces of the experience of earlier generations'. Since conventional genetic theory only allows for the inheritance of dispositions through natural selection, the idea that actual images can be passed on from generation to generation is often dismissed as a 'Lamarckian fantasy' (Gay 1989: 368). Late in his life, Freud also referred favourably to various kinds of paranormal phenomena, and observed 'that psychoanalysis, by inserting the unconscious between what is physical and what was previously called "psychical", paved the way for the assumption of such processes as telepathy' (Freud 1933: 55). This anticipates ideas that have been taken much further by contemporary writers with a transpersonal perspective, which we will examine in Chapter 7 (pp. 106–11) and Chapter 8 (pp. 137–8).

Because he saw his life as a continuous dialogue between conscious and unconscious, Jung uses the term 'unconscious' more frequently than any other major theorist. We see in Chapter 7 that not all today's transpersonal theorists share Jung's enthusiasm for the language of the unconscious. Jung would, perhaps, not have been concerned about that. Shortly before his death he read a Zen Buddhist text and told an interviewer:

> I felt as if we were talking about one and the same thing and were simply using different words for it. The use of the word 'unconscious' is not the decisive thing; what counts is the Idea that lies behind the word.
>
> (Wehr 1987: 449)

Conclusion

These accounts of the conscious and the unconscious, presented by three of the major contributors to psychodynamic approaches to psychotherapy at the beginning of the twentieth century, have each had a major influence on the subsequent development of theories of psychotherapy. We proceed to trace these, in respect of Adler in Chapter 4 (and to some extent in Chapter 6), in respect of Freud in Chapter 5 and in respect of Jung in Chapter 7.

The development of alternative discourses: Harry Stack Sullivan, Fritz Perls and Medard Boss

Many psychoanalysts who differed from Freud continued to build their theories around the technical terms that Freud had introduced. In this chapter we examine three theorists who deliberately distanced themselves from much of Freud's language, including his concept of the unconscious. Fritz Perls, Harry Stack Sullivan and Medard Boss, who were all trained in Freudian psychoanalysis (and Boss in Jungian analysis), could not accept the framework provided by Freud's topographical, economic and structural models. We can detect the direct or indirect influence of Adler in much of what they write. They share with Adler a systemic, holistic view of human life, as inextricably embedded within a matrix of multiple interactions with the natural and interpersonal world. By contrast, the discourses of Freud and his followers presented a world of rigid boundaries – between organism and environment, mind and body, conscious and unconscious – with an encapsulated, self-aware, individual at the centre.

Perls (1947: 80) speaks mockingly of an eminent analyst who 'compared the Unconscious with an elephant and the Ego with a little baby trying to lead the elephant'. He comments, 'What an isolationist conception! What a disappointment to the ambition to be omnipotent! What a split in the personality!' For Perls (1972: 35), mental, emotional and physiological activities blend into each other seamlessly. 'We are part of the universe, not separate', he observes, and our life is maintained by automatic processes of 'organismic self-regulation' (Yontef 1993: 213), which do not normally become a special focus of awareness. In the same vein, Sullivan observes that, because the view of self as separated from and set over against the world is part of a long philosophical tradition (see Chapter 2), it permeates everyday language and obscures the true nature of the relationship between individual and world. Everyday interpersonal behaviour, in which 'almost everyone deals with other people with a wonderful blend of magic, illusions and incoherent irrelevancy', sustains the 'delusion of unique individuality' (Sullivan 1937: 852) and obscures the way in which people live 'in indissoluble contact with the world of culture and of people' (Sullivan 1950: 329).

Boss also criticizes Freud for his 'far-reaching intellectual dissection' of human nature, first into 'psyche', body and external world, then into 'psychic elements', such as 'conscious' and 'unconscious', 'id', 'ego' and 'instincts' (Boss 1963: 78). He argues that Freud's account of the complex processes by which painful material is supposedly pushed into the unconscious and of how the contents of the unconscious are supposed to transform themselves symbolically into dream images are, when examined closely, logically incoherent. He cites Sartre's critique of Freud's doorkeeper model of repression (see Conkling 1986). The doorkeeper must know the characters in the anteroom pressing to get into the reception area, as otherwise he would not know whom to admit. How, then, can the individual not be aware of them too? Freud's claim that the individual remains unaware both of the repression and of the repressed material is simply a cover for self-deception. The same can be said of the dream censor who decides on how to disguise unconscious material in admitting it into figures in a dream. 'The censor can only be an unconscious consciousness', writes Boss (1977: 182), which makes no logical sense (but see Chapter 8, p. 132). Nor can Freud be defended by saying that these images are merely metaphors. What may have started as metaphor became part of a rigid propositional system (see Chapter 1). Freud's language inevitably carries with it the details of his topographical and economic theories.

Perls (1973: 55) criticizes the conceptual splitting of mind and body, 'to which the highly limited concept of the unconscious is so closely related'. He uses the example of non-verbal behaviour: when we observe a client's 'leaning forward and pushing back, his abortive kicks, his fidgets, his subtleties of enunciation, his split-second hesitations between words, his handwriting, his use of metaphor and language' (1973: 76), are we to understand them as indirect expressions of the contents of a repressed unconscious? On the contrary, writes Perls, 'all are on the surface, all are obvious, and all are meaningful'. Hillman (1997: 123), a Jungian analyst, similarly writes: 'They show in reticence, in circumlocutions and euphemisms, in shaded averted eyes, in slips, in hesitancies and gestures, second thoughts, avoidances . . . The supposedly concealed is also on view and . . . part of what any event affords to a good looker.' Boss makes the same point in describing a young woman who developed a hysterical paralysis. Daily she passed a nursery in which a handsome young gardener worked, and she found herself increasingly attracted to him. However, her parents 'were hostile to even the slightest signs of sensuality and had educated their children in an extremely prudish manner'. One day she fell over in front of the nursery and her legs became paralysed. Freud would explain this in terms of repressed libidinous strivings and instinctual images stored in the unconscious, which could only be expressed in this disguised fashion. For Boss, there is no need for speculative and unsupported hypotheses about the contents of the psyche. The girl herself was aware of her attraction to the gardener, although she had had no opportunity to reflect intellectually on it. Boss would agree with Perls that the meaning of the paralysis is 'on the surface', not hidden in the unconscious and opaque. It is simply a direct expression of her existential predicament, which

> shows that she had surrendered herself to her parents' attitude and she still existed under its spell completely. Consequently she was able to engage herself in the love relationship to the gardener only in the way of warding off her moving close to him, of stopping and blocking this movement of hers.
>
> (Boss 1963: 117–19)

These theorists' rejection of Freud's concept of the unconscious does not mean that they are not concerned about the limitations of our everyday awareness. On the contrary, these limitations interest them as much as they did Freud. We find Sullivan (1937: 856–7) writing: 'The average person magically stripped of his illusions about his friends and acquaintants would find himself surrounded by strangers'; and Perls (1972: 22) defines 'the neurotic' as 'a person who can't see the obvious, as in Andersen's fairy tale where only the child points to the obvious – that the king is naked'. In referring to 'blocking', 'stopping' and 'warding off' in his discussion of the paralysed young woman, Boss is clearly addressing the same phenomena as Freud, even though he rejects the concepts of repression and the unconscious.

Boss (1963: 101) points out that a dialectical relationship between concealment and disclosure permeates human life: 'Without concealment and darkness, man [sic] would not be the world-disclosing being that he is. Light and darkness, concealment and disclosure, belong together inseparably.' This dialectic extends to psychological theories too – they can blind and conceal as much as they enlighten and open up. Thus Sullivan (1953: 350) comments that Freud's concept of wish-fulfilment 'is misleading rather than helpful, and actually tends to limit the clarity of the psychiatrist's own thought'. Sullivan is also critical of the speculative nature of case discussions among many psychoanalysts. He read widely in social psychology and cultural anthropology and emphasizes that theory consists of hypotheses that are based on observations and must be tested against new observations. Similarly, Boss (1977: 27) notes that psycho-analysts are notorious for providing a host of speculative and incompatible interpretations of dreams whose validity their theory provided no means of establishing. By allowing themselves to be driven by theory, they 'become blind to the wealth of meaning in every phenomenon we encounter, whether waking or dreaming . . . an attachment to the banal . . . restricts their vision to seeing only impoverishment in things'.

Boss, Perls and Sullivan, like Adler, reacted against the way in which Freud's theorizing stood in the way of a holistic understanding. Their aim was to address the same territory as Freud, but to find a different discourse in which to do it, one that was faithful to their systemic perspective and the intrinsic relatedness of human life to the world at large.

Harry Stack Sullivan (1892–1949)

> You don't hear, you don't see, you don't feel, you don't observe, you don't think, you don't this and you don't that, all by the very suave manipulation of the contents of consciousness by anxiety.
>
> (Sullivan 1950: 327)

Despite Harry Stack Sullivan's attention to developing an alternative discourse, there is considerable continuity between his theories and those of Freud. As Cohen (1953: xiii) notes, several of Freud's hypotheses 'are included in his formulation such as concepts of con-scious and unconscious processes'. However, as Sullivan extends and elaborates what can be found in Freud, and as his theories provide an increasingly differentiated and subtle account of a range of psycho-logical phenomena, he increasingly distances himself from Freud's theoretical constructs. At one point, he uses the term 'conceptual unconscious', by which he means that we need to make conceptual sense of 'the discontinuities present in conscious life' (Sullivan 1950: 330). However, in his last lectures, published posthumously, Sullivan (1953) deliberately avoids the terms 'conscious' and 'unconscious'. Although the index has several entries for 'unconscious, the', when we turn to them we do not find the term 'the unconscious' at all. Instead, we read about 'covert processes' or 'the control of focal awareness'. He systematically replaces the adjective 'unconscious' with the words 'unknown', 'unnoticed', unnoted', 'overlooked' or 'unwitting', and 'conscious' is replaced by 'witting' or 'known'. On the few occasions where he uses 'conscious' or 'unconscious' he usually provides another word as well. For example, he writes that 'the genital drive is handled . . . by known – that is conscious – homosexual reveries'; or refers to 'covert processes inaccessible to awareness'; or translates, 'in other words unconscious processes, to use the old fashioned term'. Elsewhere, he writes 'only under exceptional circumstances are there reflections in consciousness – that is, in awareness' (1953: 278, 316).

Sullivan (1938) brilliantly deconstructs the details of the interpersonal processes that occur automatically in social interaction. An exchange between Mr and Mrs A, who have planned to go out for the evening, is put 'under the Sullivanian microscope' (Mullahy 1970: 289). Mrs A directs a derogatory remark at Mr A; he suddenly feels weary and no longer wants to go out. Sullivan deftly reveals layer upon layer of interlocking processes of which neither of them are aware. Mr A is unaware that Mrs A's provocation is motivated by her chronic resentment. If questioned, he would claim that such remarks by his wife are just a habit and mean nothing. Nor is he aware that his wife's remark has hurt him and evoked resentment in him, or of how his resentment 'is represented in awareness as weariness' (Sullivan 1938: 123). He also fails to recognize that in withdrawing from cooperating with their plan to go out together, he is retaliating. Sullivan suggests that Mr A's part in the interaction is governed by a 'me–you pattern', an internalized representation of himself and his wife in relationship. This is available to awareness: if questioned, Mr A will tell us that he is a contented, loving husband married to an affectionate wife who is 'uniformly amiable towards him . . . We've been married ten years and she's never found fault with me' (1938: 127). However, he is not aware that these configurations are 'illusory' and self-deceptive, and that the illusion is maintained by selectively not attending to a range of behaviours on her part that are irritating and hostile.

Mr A has another 'me–you' pattern, which features another illusory version of Mrs A that is far less benign. This is activated when a dispute about each other's friends flares up into a quarrel in which they insult and verbally attack each other. The situation escalates to the point where Mr A's

> loud-voiced anger is replaced by low-voiced rage . . . He is focally aware of his desire to strike, tear, kill the illusory Mrs A who is now before him. She is the epitome of malicious persecutions, a human viper whom the law protects . . . He says things about her which would shock him if he were to recall them when he is calm again.
>
> (Sullivan 1938: 128)

Now, although aware of his wife's anger and malice, Mr A is not aware of the shift in the governing me–you pattern; nor of the incongruity in the sudden replacement of the image of himself as affectionate, patient and respectful, by an image of himself as contemptuous and hostile. Nor is he aware of the incongruity of the similar shift in his image of his wife (from devoted and affectionate, to malicious and persecutory); or of how partial and incomplete is the current image of Mrs A to which he is responding. Even when he calms down, he will not be struck by the massive incompatibility between the experiences of self and wife mobilized by the two me–you patterns.

The situation is complicated by Mrs A's me–you patterns, which provide her own distorted images of herself and Mr A. The one portrays her as a 'tolerant wife-mother to a rather incompetent, absurdly conceited but devoted husband'; the other presents her as the 'disillusioned victim of an utterly selfish man who thinks women are inferior creatures for whose services almost anything is an extravagant overpayment' (1938: 129). Neither of them is aware of how 'a great deal of [their] interpersonal relations' is filtered through distorted cognitive systems, and involves 'operations with imaginary people' (Sullivan 1950: 329).

Sullivan's account of the developmental origins of interpersonal configurations like these has many similarities to Adler's ideas. At the root is anxiety, something that can be experienced from the very beginning of infant life in response, for example, to 'increasing tenseness and increasingly evident forbidding on the part of the mother' (Sullivan 1953: 162). Over the ensuing months, inter-personal events that induce anxiety are likely to escalate as the care-taker seeks to socialize the infant. In response, the infant begins to develop 'security operations', a wide-ranging set of covert and overt responses whose goal is to minimize or avoid experiences of anxiety induced by the caretaker's behaviour. In due course, these operations become organized into the self-system. One of the security operations is sublimation: this involves 'the unwitting substitution' for a behaviour that meets with disapproval, and thus occasions anxiety, '*of a socially more acceptable activity pattern which satisfies part of the motivational system which caused trouble*' (1953: 193; original italics). For example, an infant whose hand is soiled with faeces starts to suck its thumb. The caretaker scolds it and the child sucks a toy instead. Sullivan draws attention to the automatic character of this security operation: 'the unwitting part of it – the fact that it is not run through consciousness – is what makes it work' (Sullivan 1950: 323).

Against the background of these automatic processes, Sullivan traces the development of the capacity for awareness and intentional activity. During the juvenile period (from around age four) children move into the wider social world and the critical responses of peers, as well as of adult caretakers, put pressure on them to give up many of the ideas and operations that had been acceptable at home. In response, the self-system develops 'increasing power . . . to control focal awareness', with the result that 'what does not make sense tends to get no particular attention' (Sullivan 1953: 233). This is the beginning of 'selective inattention', which refers to the fact that 'we always overlook certain things which would be awkward if we noticed them' (Sullivan 1950: 330). This 'ever iterated miracle' becomes so pervasive that it 'covers the world like a tent' (Sullivan 1953: 374, 304) and accounts for the later difficulty in recalling events from earlier in childhood. 'Substitutive processes' are one means whereby selective inattention can be achieved. These include ' "deliberately" . . . changing the subject' of a conversation, or becoming intensely preoccupied with hypochondriacal worries, self-pitying ruminations or 'witting . . . reverie processes . . . of a compensatory character' – such as imagining that someone who had in fact rebuffed your approach had responded with interest and appreciation. All of these enable the individual to 'avoid conscious clarity about one's own situation, one's own motivations' (1953: 347, 349, 354).

In addition to the experience of anxiety, which the self-system is designed to minimize, Sullivan identifies a more intense form of emotion, which he calls 'uncanny' – an experience of intense horror or dread that is so overwhelming it cannot be integrated as an experience of 'me'. Instead it becomes the basis of 'not-me', an experience so aversive that it calls for the operation of 'certain supplementary processes which prevent one's ever discovering quite clear evidences that part of one's living is done without any awareness'. These are the processes of dissociation. Dissociation is also maintained by selective inattention processes, which ensure that it is 'practically impossible, while one is awake, to encounter uncanny emotion' (1953: 317). Thus, where an individual's hypochondriacal ideas are part of the 'precautionary apparatus' for maintaining a dissociation, they 'become extreme and absorbing' whenever interpersonal events have the effect of activating the dissociated emotion' (1953: 357). Because dissociation protects against the most extreme and unbearable emotional states, the processes of selective inattention that maintain it are much less open to investigation and insight than those that keep anxiety out of awareness.

Sullivan's central concepts illustrate his keen observation of, and detailed interest in, the limits of people's awareness of their cognitions, emotions and motivations, and the moment to moment processes of management of attention which determine what is and what is not available to awareness. We note particularly the distinctive technical terms around which he built his discourse.

Fritz Perls (1893–1970)

> In a neurosis, a part of our personality or of our potential is not available. But [Freud] said this in an odd way; he said, 'it is *in* the unconscious', as if there were such a thing as *the* unconscious rather than simply behaviour or emotions that are unknown or not available.
>
> (Perls 1972: 18–19)

Fritz Perls, the founder of Gestalt therapy, expressed his admiration for Freud by calling him 'the Livingstone of the Unconscious', and compared him to Galileo, who had 'dethroned the Earth from the centre of the Universe' (Perls 1947: 86). Nevertheless, he repeatedly presents his perspectives as a reaction to Freud, and in four lectures delivered in 1966 (Perls 1972) and in *The Gestalt Approach* (Perls 1973), which he was revising at the time of his death, the word 'unconscious' only appears when he is criticizing the traditional psychoanalytic use of the concept.

Perls's starting point is the organizational principle of figure/ ground described by the Gestalt psychologists in their investigations into human perception. If we look at a tree in a garden, it takes on a clear and organized form or 'Gestalt', and we experience it as 'figure' against the less distinct and detailed 'ground' of the rest of the garden. What we attend to, and so what becomes figure, is determined by need or motivation. When we drive through a town we do not normally notice letter boxes. 'The situation, however, changes when you have to post a letter. Then, out of an indifferently viewed background, a letter box will jump into prominence' (Perls 1947: 41). Once the letter is posted, letter boxes sink back into the ground again, and what becomes figure is determined by another need. This is a natural cycle: in response to a need something emerges as figure; focus on the figure enables us to act to satisfy the need; then the figure sinks back out of awareness. At this point, to use another Gestalt term, closure has been achieved. This means that absence of focal awareness is a natural state. It is when we are out of balance due to an unfulfilled need that something becomes the focus of awareness.

Unfortunately, when individuals attempt to fulfil their needs, they are often met with hostility, abandonment, shaming or confusing instructions like 'act your age' or 'behave yourself' (Perls 1973: 114). To cope with this, they learn to interrupt the cycle and prevent emergent needs from becoming clear figures. They therefore fail to recognize what they need and no longer get their needs met. Yontef (1993: 52) suggests that this concept of interruption of figure formation 'replaces the psychoanalytic concept of the unconscious'. It is typically referred to in such terms as 'alienation', or 'not being in touch' with significant aspects of the external world or one's 'inner life' (Yontef 1993: 146, 152); or 'disowning' or 'disavowal' of 'those aspects of our personalities which we find difficult or offensive or unattractive' (Perls 1973: 37).

It is the task of therapy to assist clients in bringing to awareness needs whose expression is being interrupted, as well as the process of interruption itself, and to direct them towards finding the resources within themselves to get those needs met in appropriate ways. Towards this end, Perls developed a technology of awareness, founded on inviting the client to keep attention on the present moment. This approach lends itself to a different metaphor: 'most psychotherapies are trying to get to the deepest depth', Perls (1972: 22) remarks. 'We are trying to get to the outermost surface.'

Such a present focus might result in awareness of some unpleasant sensation, such as a tightness in the throat; when that tightness is allowed to become 'figure' it may change into tingling sensations around the mouth and eyes; as these are attended to, what emerges as 'figure' is an impulse to burst into tears. This may be an indication of 'unfinished business'; for example, a process of mourning that has been blocked. Freud recognized that mourning is a process that calls for 'the experience and expression of the deepest emotions' (Perls 1947: 96) and that can become stalled. Perls is interested in how this interruption of the natural mourning response takes place. In response to the impulse to cry, writes Perls (1972: 19) 'we become phobic', develop an 'avoidance tendency' and direct attention elsewhere. The therapist must direct attention back to how the mourning is interrupted in the here and now so that the mourner can undo the interruptions and allow the process to take its course.

However, Perls is critical of Freud's view that the source of all present problems lies in painful situations from the past, which must be recovered and understood. He sees this as diverting attention from what the client needs to do in the here-and-now. 'We prefer to talk about the *at-this-moment-unaware*', Perls (1973: 54) remarks, and this includes a range of significant automatic processes in the present that contribute to human unhappiness. Here are four examples.

1 A man, waiting for a tram, keeps himself in an agitated state, without realizing it. Instead of occupying his mind by reading or observing what is going on around him, he repeatedly allows an image of the tram arriving to come to mind. This image activates an impulse to approach and board the tram, which has to be suppressed. The suppression produces a persistent feeling of restlessness and irritation, but the whole process takes place out of awareness and is 'automatic and unconscious' (Perls 1947: 91).

2 Emotional distress is repeatedly evoked in the present through clinging to unrealistic expectations, which individuals fail to revise, despite evidence that they are not reality based. Such people, comments Perls (1947: 97), 'are not prepared to see the fundamental mistake of expecting that reality should coincide with our wishes'.

3 Individuals with 'anticipatory neurosis' are unaware that their main problem is the energy they invest in wasteful and ineffective worrying. They maintain a chronically anxious state, by worrying about how they will handle the situation they will be confronted with in a few hours' time. They do not even carry out in the present situation what they planned to do when worrying about it a few hours beforehand, so they 'never collect the fruits of their efforts, as their plans never make contact . . . with reality' (Perls 1947: 95).

4 Perls (1973: 46) also addresses patterns of interpersonal interaction that have become 'so habitual that the neurotic is no longer aware of them', although he does not provide the kind of detailed analysis that we find in Sullivan. These self-defeating 'interpersonal manoeuvres' fail, even if successful, to meet the individual's real needs. One task of therapy, therefore, is to bring these processes to awareness as a first step towards working on meaningful change.

Perls (1972: 20) conceptualizes the development of maturity in terms of a progressive shift from 'environmental support' (as offered by parents and caretakers) towards 'self-support' and towards accepting responsibility for the consequences of one's behaviours, including those that are automatic and habitual. Perls believes that, unless the uncovering of pain from the past is balanced by active movement towards a more independent and mature mode of functioning, therapy only reinforces the client's 'childishness and dependency'. We are infantile because we are afraid to take responsibility in the now, writes Perls (1972: 20). Clients are not aware of how they fail to take responsibility for their actions, so therapists must draw this to their attention and encourage them to change their approach actively, and to learn to draw on their own self-support in getting their needs met.

Like Rogers (see Example 4 in Chapter 1, pp. 6–7), Perls believes that healthy functioning involves an organismic, holistic and immediate way of living in the world. All individuals have the potential for this kind of living, but this potential often fails to develop (due to the kinds of processes described above). The most important aim of therapy, therefore, involves

> uncovering our own ability . . . our own eyes, in order to find our potential, to see what is going on, to discover how we can enlarge our lives, to find means at our disposal that will let us cope with a difficult situation.
>
> (Perls 1972: 21)

This involves a radical transformation of consciousness, a kind of awakening to a new way of being, which Perls (1972: 44) captures in the famous maxim: 'Lose your mind and come to your senses.'

Medard Boss (1903–91)

Our being-in-the-world reveals itself as the holding open [of] . . . a
realm of openness to the world, of the ability to perceive the
significances of that which encounters us spreading out world-
wide.

(Boss 1986: 246)

Medard Boss draws on the phenomenological philosophy of Husserl
and Heidegger to offer a distinctive psychological discourse within
which the nature, achievements and limitations of human experience
can be addressed. Whether we are aware of it or not, he points out,
the network of relationships within which our lives are situated
makes an impact on us. Many of these relationships are aspects of
the existential conditions of life. We are located in space physically
further from or nearer to specific people or places, which renders
them more or less accessible to us. We are deeply affected by the past
and inevitably oriented towards possibilities (feared or hoped for)
in the future – for example, this relationship will change if we learn
that an economic depression is looming, or that there is a risk of a
widespread nuclear war. We are embodied – we do not just happen
to inhabit a body that we can enter and leave as we please. So our
relationship to our body will change as, for example, we enter
puberty, become pregnant, lose our hair or become diseased. We are
born, grow, develop and die, and as we go through life we will have
changing relationships to the phase of life we are in, the phase of life
we are moving towards and the inevitability of death. These relationships are so many and complex that we cannot be fully aware of the
implications of all of them at once. Nevertheless, it is part of human
nature to be open to the implications of all relationships, whether we
actively reflect on them or not.

For Boss (1963: 80), the essential feature of human nature is its
'meaning-disclosing, elucidating character', which exists as 'a unique
illuminating realm of understanding openness spanning an entire
world' (Boss 1977: 185). As human beings, we are capable of 'per-
ceiving the encountered fully, thinking of it, reflecting upon it,
feeling it with all the richness of one's own selfhood, and of taking
action accordingly'. Although these meanings 'claim our existence',
they do not usually present themselves in a ready made verbal
formulation. For the young woman whose legs became paralysed
(discussed above, p. 51), the meaning of her relationship with the
handsome young gardener presented itself as a growing confusion

and uneasiness, which culminated in her paralysis. As her interest had been stirred by her repeated encounters with him, 'her entire existence had become involved in this relation of emotional attraction . . . [which had taken] complete possession of her existence'. But, although the relationship impacted on her so powerfully, it was not one she could talk about or even reflect on, because she was 'under the spell' of her parents' 'prohibiting attitude'. At this stage, she 'could not even think: "It is not permitted to love the man erotically." ' However, the three years of psychoanalysis that followed provided her with a context in which that kind of reflection and articulation could take place. In due course, this enabled her to 'mature into a human freedom which, for the first time in her life, opened up her existence to the possibility of thinking and feeling a loving attraction towards a man' (1977: 118, 119). To understand the case, writes Boss, there is no need to explain the woman's predicament in terms of conflict between psychic elements such as 'id' and 'superego', or by speculation about thoughts and 'strivings' repressed in the unconscious. Indeed, Boss tells us that the material of this therapy provided no evidence for such repressed material. His account in terms of a phenomenological discourse is faithful to the woman's experience before the therapy and as it unfolded during it.

Dreaming is another mode in which our relationships with aspects of the world disclose themselves. 'Often enough a person is exposed to unfamiliar significances *for the first time ever* while dreaming' (1977: 214, original emphasis). This means that a dream, like the woman's paralysed legs, provides an invitation to look at and reflect on what is being disclosed. This is illustrated in Boss's discussion of a young military recruit who dreamed he was running away, as fast as he could, from a giant: 'but the distance between us keeps getting smaller. Soon . . . he actually steps on me . . . so I am wedged between his toes. It's just a matter of seconds before he squashes me altogether' (1977: 42). For Boss, the images of the dream are not 'symbols' that point in a veiled way to something 'in the unconscious', such as his father, some authority figure or the therapist. The figures are what they are (a giant gaining ground on a tiny, terrified man). Boss can find no reason why, if the dreams concern his father, his father should not appear, as fathers (and mothers) often do in dreams. Nor does the dream portray, in disguise, repressed drives and impulses that need to be uncovered for the dream to be explained. Instead, the dream can serve as a tool for confronting the young man with aspects of his existential situation that he is not attending to.

Boss focuses on the mood or 'attunement' of the dream, for this holds the key to the meanings waiting to be disclosed. In this case, it is a state of 'panicked anxiety about death'. The dreamer has every reason to be anxious. Recently recruited into the army, he has suddenly shifted from a relatively comfortable life to subordination to strict discipline within a powerful military hierarchy. This attunement, which was 'not adequately wakingly admitted', can 'call forth dream beings and events that correspond to it'. It erupts into the dream world through the vivid image of the giant chasing the tiny man. Should the recruit tell the dream to a therapist, it is likely that he will no longer be able to 'overlook' (a term often used by Sullivan, too) the presence of this mood as a component of his waking experience. Another aspect of the young man's life is that he has never yet seen himself as a grown man, able to exercise power and authority. This is an as yet 'unrealized existence'. On the basis of this dream, a therapist might say to him, 'While dreaming, you saw adult manhood only in the form of a strange giant who threatened your life. Now that you are awake, do you begin to see that the same sort of adult manhood also exists as a possibility in your own life?' (1977: 47, 48).

The dream enables the therapist to draw attention to emotional responses to situations or relationships that are still prereflective, and to the potential for more differentiated, subtle, vital and authentic ways of being in relationship than the individual has as yet realized. Sometimes, this may be accomplished through the therapist's merely describing the images and emotional states of the dream. Where these insights are not easily integrated, the therapist may need to be persistent in confronting the dreamer with them again and again. Boss calls this work 'explication'. He deliberately avoids the term 'interpretation', because it has become inextricably linked to psychoanalytic methods that involve identifying symbolic references to parental figures, sexual organs, wish fulfilments and forbidden impulses, and looking for clues to these in the dream images and in other images brought to awareness by free association. He is cautious about free association itself, because, far from being a sure pathway into the unconscious, it can just as easily throw up images and thoughts that distract attention away from the existential meaning of the dream.

Where Freud posits two separate realms, 'the conscious' and 'the unconscious', Boss describes a dialectical relationship between what is disclosed to the 'worldopenness' of an individual's experience and what remains concealed from it. For Boss (1977: 183), Freud's 'unconscious' is a subjective descendent – distant, abstract, anthropomorphized, objectified – of that prehuman, in fact, preontological concealment from which every human existence must wrest a region of illumination from the world.

From this perspective, what is surprising is not that things are out of awareness, but that our awareness can comprehend them. The 'illumination' that is human awareness is an achievement which Boss (1977: 189) likens to a 'clearing in a forest, a free and open area that has been wrested from, and must constantly be defended against, darkness and concealment'.

The vast richness of all that exists, with its complex network of relationships and existential possibilities, is termed 'Beingness'. The subtlety and wonder of a human being's meaning-disclosing relationship with 'Beingness' is distorted or lost in the rigid language of Freud's propositional models. Commenting on the giant in the dream discussed above, Boss (1977: 44) asks:

> Where do giants originate, then, if not in the interior of the human 'psyche'? . . . Answer: out of Be-ingness as such, i.e. out of that great darkness that rules all that is, heaven and earth, God and man, and out of which these things 'come to light'. Compared to the grandeur of that darkness, all notions of an endopsychic 'unconscious' whether individual or collective, seem the gross distortions of a subjective reductionism.

Conclusion

Each of these three theorists might have aligned himself with Merleau-Ponty's (1942: 173) observation that 'consciousness is a network of significant intentions which are sometimes clear to themselves and sometimes on the contrary lived rather than known'. Although offering rather different perspectives, what they have in common is that they deliberately distanced themselves from Freud by avoiding the language of the unconscious and creating an alternative discourse. In Chapter 1, we observed that Freud's conceptualization of the unconscious as a 'region' is often targeted by critics who are concerned about the implications of the spatial metaphor. However, it is not the spatiality of the metaphor that is the main problem for Perls, Sullivan and Boss. They are all quite comfortable using spatial metaphors when it suits them. For example, Boss uses the image of making a clearing in the forest and actively defending it against encroachment; Perls (1972: 23) describes the process of therapy as taking the client through 'the five layers of neurosis'; and Sullivan (1953: 145) refers to 'good-me', 'bad-me' and 'not-me' as 'areas' of personality. By distancing themselves from Freud, they are able to look anew at questions about the scope and limitations of awareness in everyday life. To a greater or lesser degree, they each extend the critique of Freud offered by Adler. We see this in Perls's emphasis on automatic, habitual processes, and the shifting of material in and out of awareness; in Sullivan's accounts of interpersonal patterns, unwittingly played out; and in Boss's insights into how something may be experienced but not reflected on and articulated in language. We will see in Chapter 5 how these insights are taken up by psycho-analytic theorists of a later generation, many of whom reshape Freud's ideas considerably, but remain comfortable with giving 'the unconscious' a significant place in their discourse.

CHAPTER 5

Evolving psychoanalytic discourses of the unconscious

> [Freud's] discoveries of the survival of childhood experiences in the adult unconscious and of the phenomenon of repression have influenced my life and my way of thinking. However, I have come to conclusions today different from those Freud reached over eighty years ago.
>
> (Miller 1984: viii)

Psychoanalytic thinking has come a long way since Freud. In this chapter we examine the way in which unconscious processes are conceptualized within contemporary psychoanalytic discourse. The development of psychotherapy among those who see their work as having continuity with Freud's has been a complex process. Consequently, the groupings of psychotherapists who call themselves 'psychoanalytic' are quite diverse. We therefore select as a representative sample writers who would situate themselves within self psychology (Kohut 1977), object relations theory (Kernberg 1976; Bollas 1987; Summers 1999) and relational psychoanalysis (Mitchell and Aron 1999). Despite the diversity, there is much common ground theoretically, in three important areas: (a) the processes of infant and child development; (b) the significance of an interpersonal perspective for an understanding of self and of the therapy process; (c) the nature of the dialectic between conscious and unconscious processes. These developments have led to the replacement of Freud's formal theories by some very different discourses of the unconscious.

Interpersonal schemas and the developmental process

Like Sullivan, these theorists recognize that significant emotional experiences are organized around schematic representations of self and other, which have their origins in infancy. Mahler's (1979) separation–individuation theory, based on observation of infants and young children, describes the developmental processes that take place in the first three years of life. Kernberg (1987) discusses how the child's consciousness evolves (and with that the capacity for unconscious processes) as the stages described by Mahler unfold. In the symbiotic phase, in the first months of life, the infant's awareness is based on inborn cognitive–affective schemas that do not yet provide a separate representation of self and other, so that experiences of self and mother are fused. Within a few months, the infant is able to symbolize these interpersonal events in the form of images, which include pleasurable images of 'good self–good mother' and emotionally distressing images of 'bad self–bad mother' (1987: 10). The process of separation–individuation begins at around five months, with the 'hatching' phase. Infants develop a cohesive body image that provides a structure for integrating the varying proprioceptive (bodily) experiences that occur during different activities and in different affective states. They become aware that 'good self–good mother' and 'bad self–bad mother' experiences have a common element. They develop self-awareness, and recognize themselves as an autonomous 'seat of consciousness' that can experience different experiential states. They may begin to attribute awareness and emotional states to others as well.

Next comes the 'practising' stage: the child who can now crawl, and later walk, makes increasingly longer exploratory forays away from the mother. If mother is available and supportive, this confronts the infant with its separateness in doses that are tolerable and offer a sense of adventure. However, self is still only represented in relation to object (e.g. mother), in the form of 'self-object' schemas. Where mother appears as a safe, invulnerable figure, toddlers have a false sense of security, are unaware of their dependence and helplessness and perceive self and mother as omnipotent and having magical powers. At around 18 months, the 'rapprochement crisis' occurs as they confront the meaning of their alternating 'moving away from the mother and returning to her for emotional refueling' (Horner 1987: 35). They recognize their own helplessness and dependency, and shame is experienced, in stark contrast to feelings of omnipotence. Over the next 18 months or so, the 'good self–good mother' and 'bad self–bad mother' schemas are restructured to provide separate schemas for self and other. Children recognize that 'good self' experiences and 'bad self' experiences both belong to them. If this developmental phase is negotiated successfully, they attain 'full continuity of self-awareness' (Kernberg 1987: 11), and enter childhood with a secure and cohesive sense of self, a sense of excitement and enthusiasm about their ability to make their way in the social world and a sense of trust in their affective states as a guide to decision-making and relating to others. The foundation is laid for authentic engagement with life and healthy personality development (Summers 1999).

Development derailed: character defence

For this to occur, the caretaker must provide a natural and spontaneous interaction with the infant in terms of eye contact, handling and active responding to the child's behaviour, vocalizations and emotional states. This is referred to as 'good-enough mothering' (Winnicott 1965: 145), 'attuned responsiveness' (Stolorow and Atwood 1999: 368) or 'an optimal zone of affective responsiveness' (Summers 1999: 52). Where caregivers are unthreatened by children's varying emotional states, and can respond to them in a way that acknowledges them, children can develop a sense of agency in relationship, and learn how to regulate their emotions and integrate them into their growing sense of self.

This developmental process becomes derailed by 'the mother's inability to sense her infant's needs' (Winnicott 1965: 145), or her subjecting the infant to neglect, rejection, abandonment, inconsistency, shaming, hostility or other excessive or misguided responses. These evoke confusing and painful emotional states that infants are ill-equipped to deal with. To protect themselves, they may sacrifice spontaneous self-expression in favour of an inauthentic mode of relating, which enables them to maintain themselves in relationship with their caretakers, despite the emotional pain they are exposed to. Ferenczi (1929: 124) wrote of 'the greater part of the personality becom[ing] . . . a *teratoma* [tumour], the task of adaptation to reality being shouldered by the fragment of the personality that has been spared'. This has affinities with the metaphor of the replacement of the true self by a false self (Winnicott 1965), which, in turn, has obvious affinities with Adler's 'guiding fiction' or 'neurotic modus vivendi', Jung's 'persona', Sullivan's 'self-system', the traditional psychoanalytic concept of 'character defence' (Summers 1999) and Berne's (1975) 'adapted child', which displaces the 'free child'. However it is spoken about, most theorists would agree with Summers (1999: 69), that 'burial of authentic self potential' means that 'movement towards self realization is crippled'.

Repression and dissociation: two metaphors for the roots of the unconscious

Two widely used metaphors play a prominent role in referring to the limited awareness people have of significant aspects of their psychological life. The first, dissociation, implies that two or more separate self-systems alternate in controlling consciousness and behaviour. We find this in Janet's theory of the splitting off of 'subconscious fixed ideas' (Chapter 2, pp. 26–7), and in Breuer and Freud's references to 'splitting' (Chapter 3, p. 29). Freud (1910: 19) observed how a single person can have

> several different mental groupings, which can remain more or less independent of one another, which can 'know nothing' of one another and which can alternate with one another in their hold upon consciousness.

Jung (1948: 97, 98) used the language of the 'feeling-toned complex', which he likened to a 'fragmentary personality' or 'splinter psyche', which can bring about an 'unconscious alteration of personality known as identification with the complex'. Freud (1927: 156) also identified another kind of splitting that occurred 'in the ego'. In two cases of boys who had lost their fathers during childhood, he noted that 'one current of their mental life . . . had not recognized their father's death'. He called this 'disavowal'. However, 'there was another current which took full account of that fact. The attitude which fitted in with the wish [that the father were still alive] and the attitude which fitted in with reality existed side by side.'

The second metaphor, that of repression, implies that a consciously aware self-organization excludes from awareness material that is emotionally disturbing. In Freud, what were repressed were the two instinctual drives, aggression and libido. Later theorists, recognizing the wide range of emotional states that can be repressed, preserved Freud's view of the primacy of the drives by referring to these emotions as 'drive derivatives'. Kernberg maintains this language, although he observes that 'we never observe pure drives in clinical practice, but only drive invested object relations' (Kernberg 1987: 4). For this reason, many contemporary theorists (e.g. Summers 1999) abandon Freud's drive terminology altogether and consider that what are repressed are schematic configurations associated with distressing emotions that are evoked by everyday interpersonal events.

Although Freud addressed aspects of dissociation, his topographical model gives pride of place to the exclusion of unwanted material beneath a 'repression barrier'. Kohut (1977) integrates the two concepts; he suggests that dissociation and repression are two discrete mechanisms, which he calls the 'horizontal split' (repression) and the 'vertical split' (dissociation). This is illustrated in the self structure of a 'Mr X': there is a vertical split, with a grandiose and superior self on one side; on the other side are two further parts, a 'depressed, empty self' horizontally split from 'an incompletely organized nuclear self' that it represses (1977: 213). Goldberg (1999) takes up Kohut's language of the vertical and horizontal split and examines how the vertical split underlies a range of personality and behaviour disorders.

However, the terms repression and dissociation are not always used rigorously to refer to distinct mechanisms; instead, they can be seen as metaphors that at times converge and at times capture different aspects of the multiplicity and inconsistency of human experience, behaviour and self-presentation. In discussing a dream, Ferenczi (1931: 135) applies both ideas: he refers to 'the splitting of the self into a suffering, brutally destroyed part, and a part that, as it were, knows everything but feels nothing'; but then he refers to the action of the latter on the former as 'primal repression'. Sullivan uses the term 'dissociation' for a mechanism that looks like a horizontal split. He distinguishes between 'bad-me' and 'not-me' experiences and refers to 'not-me' experiences as dissociated. Nevertheless, both are subject to exclusion from awareness by the same security operations, especially selective inattention; in the case of 'not-me' the security operations are applied with much greater intensity (see Chapter 4, pp. 55–6). Vertical splitting appears in Sullivan's descriptions of parallel representations of self and other in relationship.

This is also a central feature of object relations theory. Fairbairn, for example, described three parallel self-schemas that appear in infants in response to different interpersonal situations: the central ego in response to being unconditionally loved; the libidinal ego in response to mother being present but not sufficiently available (the 'teasing mother'); and the anti-libidinal ego in response to mother being hostile or rejecting (Grotstein and Rinsley 1994). This theory also describes how, in due course, emotionally painful self-schemas are repressed, even though they may be activated by interpersonal situations later in life, and give rise to the distinctive emotions associated with them. It thus includes both vertical and horizontal splitting.

Kernberg (1976) sees vertical splitting as the more primitive process: early infancy is characterized by a normal splitting of 'good-self' and 'bad-self' experiences, which, in due course, are integrated into a single self-schema. However, integration of bad-self experiences that are intensely painful is not possible and the two images remain apart. By the end of the second year, the capacity for repression emerges and replaces splitting as the main means of defence. This coincides with the development of the false self, which may furnish the outward appearance of consistency. The split between false and true self is therefore conceived of as a horizontal, rather than a vertical, split. Where early splitting is unresolved, individuals fail to develop a cohesive sense of self and display marked inconsistency of mood as they shift dramatically from one ego state to another. In therapy, for example, a client may idealize and almost worship the therapist on one occasion, and on another be hostile and contemptuous. There is no central self that can recognize how unrealistic the idealization is, or that can take responsibility for the hostile behaviour that is exhibited in the contemptuous ego state.

Dissociation, multiplicity and fragmentation

For some 150 years, it has been widely recognized that the most dramatic dissociative processes are set in motion by traumatic events, in particular emotional, physical and sexual abuse. Freud, apparently succumbing to social pressure, changed his views about the role of infantile and childhood trauma, and concluded that the *majority* of emotionally charged images from dreams or free association were the product of fantasy and were not the result of trauma. Ferenczi (1929: 121–2), whose 'neocathartic method' often led him to observe clients re-experiencing early childhood trauma, remained at odds with Freud on this matter. In response to trauma, he concluded, a '*splitting off* of a part of the personality occurs [which] lives on hidden, ceaselessly endeavouring to make itself felt, without finding any outlet except in neurotic symptoms' (original italics). As already noted, Ferenczi also uses the metaphor of repression, referring to the split-off part as the 'repressed part of the personality'. He also describes how the therapist can contact the split-off infant or child part and 'persuade it to engage in what I might almost call an infantile conversation'.

Echoing Ferenczi's conclusions some sixty years later, Davies and Frawley (1999: 281) describe how survivors of infantile or childhood trauma

> erect the semblance of a functioning, adaptive, interpersonally related self around the screaming core of a wounded and abandoned child . . . [but] the abused child . . . lives on, searching still for acknowledgement, validation, and compensation.

They decry the 'psychoanalytic politics' that resulted in attempts by Freud and his followers to discredit Ferenczi with regard to the reality of abuse memories. Taking the same view, Miller (1984) argues that several of Freud's later conceptualizations were rationalizations for his denial of the significance of childhood trauma. Therapists who believe that memories of abuse are products of infantile fantasy need a complex array of constructs to account for the material that emerges. Concepts such as infantile sexuality, the death instinct and conflicts between social requirements and 'drives' turn out to be obscure and obfuscating once it is recognized that what are emerging are general or specific memories of actual abusive events.

For Davies and Frawley, what is kept out of awareness is a complex structure, like another person. This 'fully developed . . . rather primitively organized alternative self' has been 'cordoned off and isolated', and may only hitherto have expressed itself indirectly through such symptoms as disruptive behaviour, sudden emotional outbursts or depressive episodes. In therapy, the client may feel as if a new voice is beginning to speak up, someone who feels like a stranger. The therapist allows the buried abused child self to begin to tell his or her story and let his or her feelings be heard and acknowledged for the first time. The therapist may also notice that the client shifts gear as the split-off child expresses itself through 'a subtle change in vocabulary, grammar, body postures and movements' (Davies and Frawley 1999: 284). It is as if there are two people in treatment: an adult struggling to cope and an abused child struggling to be heard. In cases where there have been repeated traumas, there may be several 'inner children', each with its own story of trauma and unexpressed feelings. Therapy therefore involves contacting and working with 'old selves' that have been 'dissociatively (or dynamically) foreclosed' or 'defensively disavowed' (Davies 1998: 196). Davies (1998: 201, 205) prefers to 'replace the concept of repression with that of dissociation', but sees a continuum of dissociation. At one end is 'multiplicity', where the client can be asked to allow the split-off part to express itself, but is also able to stand outside, observe and reflect on what is expressed. At the other end is 'fragmentation', where the split-off part completely takes over and there is no reflective awareness on the part of the client with regard to what is happening. At its most extreme, in dissociative identity disorder, different identities take over at different times, with some identities having no knowledge of the others and therefore no access to the memories of what they did (see Example 7 in Chapter 1, p. 9).

'The unconscious' in contemporary psychoanalytic discourse

As a result of these developments, psychoanalytic psychotherapy is understood to involve much more than 'making the unconscious conscious' (Kohut 1977: 210). For Kohut (1977), the goal of therapy is 'the restoration of the self'; for Horner (1987: 38), it is 'the repair of the defects of character, of the unconscious representational world'; for Summers (1999: 104), it is 'the relinquishment of current object relations and their replacement by new, more authentic ways of relating'. These are ambitious aims and, to achieve them, a great deal that is out of awareness needs to be brought to light. However, Freud's classic topographical and structural models have largely given way to new conceptual frameworks and language. Nevertheless, the historical precedent of using phrases which have the form 'the . . . unconscious' dies hard (a point we explore further in Chapter 8). Stolorow and Atwood (1999) continue this tradition by defining 'three realms of the unconscious': the *prereflective unconscious*, the *dynamic unconscious* and the *unvalidated unconscious*. The spatial connotations of the term 'realm' are only to be taken metaphorically, since what in effect they discuss are three ways in which the kind of material that is investigated in psychotherapy gets to be out of awareness.

The dynamic unconscious

The concept of a *dynamic* unconscious has been prevalent since the nineteenth century (Chapters 2 and 3), although not necessarily with that name. For Stolorow and Atwood (1999: 368), it covers the same territory as it did for Freud; it results from the 'defensive walling off

of . . . memories, fantasies, feelings, and other experiential contents
. . . because of their association with emotional conflict and subjective
danger'. However, they are at pains to strip the concept of the 'meta-
psychological encumbrances' of classical Freudian theory. There are
several important aspects to this reconceptualization.

First, the dynamic unconscious is formed and maintained within
significant relationships. Children keep out of awareness painful
states that threaten the relationship with caretakers on whom they
depend. What are repressed, therefore, are relational configurations
associated with painful emotional states. Kernberg believes that the
first stage in the development of the repressed unconscious begins
during the symbiotic stage, when the self is still represented in terms
of fused self-other images. As infants explore and interact with the
world around them, less emotionally intense self–other images
become integrated into infants' reality-based schemas. At the same
time, self–other images associated with intense states of, for example,
abandonment, frustration, fear and rage 'separate out into a deep
layer of fantastic imagery' (Kernberg 1987: 10).

Second, Freud's idea of a fixed 'repression barrier' between *Cs* and
Ucs has been replaced by a concept closer to Sullivan's view that what
is available to awareness is determined moment to moment by the
dynamic activity of security operations that maintain selective
inattention. Thus Stolorow and Atwood (1999: 369) observe that
'the boundary between conscious and unconscious is revealed to be
a fluid and ever-shifting one'. This is partly because one person's
defensiveness is determined at any moment by the defensiveness of
the other. Where individuals expect that painful emotional states will
be unacceptable to those with whom they are currently in relationship and will threaten the sustainability of interpersonal contact,
repression is maintained. Where the other is attuned, responsive,
empathic and accepting, the opportunity arises to feel and express
what could not be expressed before.

Also similar to Sullivan is Kernberg's (1987: 4) recognition of
'a dynamic layering' of defensive activity. Nearer the surface are
defensive processes, which shift their character according to the
interpersonal context. The deeper layers contain material that
Sullivan termed dissociated: intensely charged primitive images of
the first few months of life, and the systems that developed to
keep them repressed, where, as Kernberg (1987: 4) puts it, there is
'a merging of the deepest layers of defensive operations with aspects
of the id'.

A further difference from Freud is that many contemporary

theorists do not see Freud's primary process, with its primitive and irrational mode of processing information, as characteristic of the dynamic unconscious. 'From an object relations point of view', Horner (1987: 30) remarks, 'the unconscious is highly organized, being characterized by a discoverable structure, with its own dynamics, comparable to the dynamics of conscious experience.' Kernberg (1987: 4), though closer to Freud, also observes that 'the repressed unconscious . . . has more structure than is implied by its primary process character . . . what we observe are repressed internalized object relations'. Epstein (1998: 103) provides a helpful perspective: he suggests that, rather than being an accurate account of unconscious processing in general, Freud's description of primary process is a characterization of particular altered states of consciousness – 'a degraded form of experiential processing that is useful for understanding dreams . . . delusions and hallucinations'.

A final and particularly marked difference from Freud is found in theorists who conceptualize therapy as recovering and nurturing 'the hidden core of the true self' (Hirsch and Roth 1995: 266), and who conceptualize the dynamic unconscious in terms not as much of unfulfilled wishes as of unrealized potentials. The authentic desires of the 'buried self', argues Summers (1999: 65), 'continue to seek indirect modes of expression, which we call symptoms'. This means that problematic behaviours and emotions, such as chronic procrastination or outbursts of uncharacteristic rage, can be understood as the true self expressing itself in veiled form. Rage, rather than being repressed infantile aggression, may be the only authentic way individuals have found to express their sense of being abused and taken for granted. Similarly, procrastination over one's studies, rather than being self-punitive, may be the only authentic expression students have found for their resentment at having to live out life plans made for them by their parents.

Unconscious but not repressed: the prereflective unconscious

Stolorow and Atwood (1999: 367, 370) define the prereflective unconscious as 'the organizing principles that unconsciously shape and thematize a person's experiences'. This picks up a number of perspectives that are captured by Romanyshyn's (1982: 93) observation that 'unconsciousness is the absence of reflections' (see Chapter 1, p. 3). Freud's recognition of the importance of reflective awareness is incorporated in his structural model (see Chapter 3, pp. 33–4), which recognized that there is an unconscious aspect to the ego 'which produces powerful effects . . . and which requires special work before it can be made conscious' (Freud 1923a: 17). These defensive processes, as well as the internalized rules of the superego, are unconscious but not repressed. In their different ways, Adler, Sullivan and Perls draw attention to automatic psychological processes that individuals have no insight into, and that create problems for them and those around them. In contemporary psychoanalysis, it is understood that, without realizing it, individuals act under the influence of relational schemas that have not developed in an integrated way to full maturity because of the failure to negotiate the passage from symbiosis to separation/ individuation in a healthy manner. A central aspect of therapy is the bringing to awareness of the detailed processes that characterize current relational patterns and the investigation of how they interfere with spontaneous responsiveness and result in chronically unsatisfactory interpersonal relationships. Since these are enacted in the relationship with the therapist, therapists can guide clients in elucidating the 'preformed meanings and invariant themes' under whose influence their 'experience of the analytic situation is unconsciously and recurrently patterned' (Stolorow and Atwood 1999: 371).

Related to this is the role of compensatory character defences in shaping the client's style of interaction. Summers (1999: 71) describes a client whose 'haughty, arrogant attitude . . . served as a character defence against her feelings of shame and inadequacy', and notes how this had the effect of 'distancing her even further from emotional connections with others'. Here, the therapist's task is to help the client to see how the 'arrogant attitude' stands in the way of her engaging in meaningful relational interactions, as well as to gain insight into why she assumed it in the first place. This conceptualization appropriates central features of Adler's ideas, and his speaking of automatic processes that are 'hidden' and 'not understood' (Chapter 3) is an obvious anticipation of the prereflective unconscious. Like the dynamic unconscious, Stolorow and Atwood (1999: 367, 371) observe, this kind of material 'can be made conscious only with great effort' and 'psychoanalysis is, above all else, a method for illuminating the prereflective unconscious'.

Another aspect of the prereflective unconscious is elucidated by feminist psychoanalytic therapists. They argue that, at the end of the rapprochement phase, children confront the existential conflict between relationship and agency: to be active in the world and pursue independent goals, sacrifices must be made in the area of relationships; to maintain and enrich relationships, sacrifices must be made in the area of agency. This conflict is resolved by socializing males to focus on agency at the expense of relationship and females to focus on relationship at the expense of agency. For Layton (1998: 45), however, this is not a gentle acculturation, but a 'violent imposition' of a 'dictum of what girls and boys are not allowed to do'. It lays the foundation for unsatisfying relational patterns and distressing emotional predicaments in the future. Women seek to restore their lost agency by finding an idealized man; he inevitably disappoints since he cannot restore her agency, and, being relationally crippled, cannot meet her needs for intimacy. Men immerse themselves in autonomous activity to compensate for the loss of 'the primary relatedness they had with mother', but are constantly threatened by their unacknowledged dependency and longing for relationship. To restore the balance, they seek an idealized woman; but she, rather than restoring his lost relational capacity, is frustrated by his relational limitations, and instead of being consistently nurturing, complains of loneliness and visits him with resentment.

Traditionally, the internalized imperatives that set up these patterns are attributed to the superego, a psychological structure that records familial and cultural norms and automatically moulds our behaviour to them throughout life. However, Layton considers it misleading to think that these predicaments are produced by rules 'inside' individuals. Instead, they originate from a wider socio-cultural matrix that is permeated by a complex network of ideological control mechanisms that maintain the values of 'hegemonic masculinity and femininity' (Layton 1998: 45). These values are regularly enacted in everyday patterns of behaviour, at home, at work and in the media; unwittingly, individuals observe them, imitate them, identify with them, live by them, model them for others; they also enforce them by punishing, despising and shaming those who deviate from them. Layton (1999) calls this the 'normative unconscious', and conceptualizes it systemically as inside us, outside us and all around (see Example 9 in Chapter 1, p. 12).

These patterns cannot be understood without bringing to light the nature and impact of the gendered cultural assumptions within which individuals are embedded, and they cannot be changed without political activity. The work of bringing them to awareness and of challenging them is often called 'consciousness-raising', a term that refers to the bringing to awareness of aspects of the prereflective unconscious. It is also called 'conscientizing', which refers more specifically to bringing to light hidden relationships of unequal power. Layton points to the difficulties involved in overcoming these kinds of hidden assumptions. Feminists often promote new definitions of gender identity in a spirit of disdain and domination, which 'tend[s] to exclude as well as include' (Layton 1998: 2). This is because the new definitions often unconsciously embody their promoters' hidden assumptions and unconscious distortions of the needs and values of others.

The unvalidated unconscious and unformulated experience

The *unvalidated* unconscious refers to 'experiences that could not be articulated because they never evoked the requisite validating responses' (Stolorow and Atwood 1999: 370). Boss's discussion of the case of a paralysed young woman (see pp. 51 and 60–1) provides an example of this. He attributed her paralysis not to repression, but to the fact that she had not had the opportunity to reflect on and articulate her attraction towards the gardener with whom she was in love. We discussed above how the quality of responsiveness that infants receive from their caretakers determines whether they learn to differentiate their own needs, emotions and motivations, and in due course to name them. Experiential states become fully conscious as they become part of the shared consensual field created by social interaction through language; where they do not receive such acknowledgement and validation they remain unarticulated and are effectively disowned. This is the basis of the unvalidated unconscious.

'We all live in an unconscious world which has much in common with that of the infant', suggests McIntosh (1995: 35). Similarly, Adler (1938: 16) observed that much of our formative early experience 'has never been comprehended in words' (see Chapter 3, p. 41); and Sullivan (1950: 317) that 'we note many things which we do not formulate; that is about which we do not develop clear ideas about what happened to us'. Stern (1997: 79) takes up Sullivan's use of the term 'formulate': 'When a patient is finally able to think about a previously unaccepted part of life, seldom are fully formulated thoughts simply waiting to be discovered, ready for exposition. Instead, what is usually experienced is a kind of confusion.' This represents emergent experience that has failed to make the journey to full articulation in language. Until it can do so, it remains 'unformulated experience'.

A young man who presented with panic attacks provides another example of experience that is unformulated because it is not validated (Goldberg 1999). His parents had miscalculated in planning to provide for the education of him and his older brother. They decided to take out a loan, which he would have to pay back in due course himself. The panic attacks had begun soon after they had informed him of this. After a few sessions of therapy, what emerged was a huge rage he felt towards them. He felt deeply betrayed, but he also felt 'the implicit parental demand' for these feelings 'to be ignored or at least not to be psychologically reckoned with'. As a result, suggests Goldberg (1999: 142), 'the material of resentment is not repressed or suppressed but rather lives on in a different place'. Until he entered therapy there was no one to validate his betrayal and resentment. They were 'disavowed'; that is, vertically rather than horizontally split off from his validated experience. At first he experienced confusion when these feelings were validated by the therapist; in due course, however, he could allow himself to see them as reasonable and natural reactions to what his parents had done.

In the complex process of growing up, children often find themselves in situations in which the conditions are not met for them to give clear and conscious articulation of their experience. They may simply give up on the process because caregivers respond in a shaming or punitive way. Miller (1984: 18) uses the term 'poisonous pedagogy' to refer to a child-rearing attitude 'which attempts to suppress all vitality, creativity and feeling in the child'. One effect of this, she observes, is that 'early traumatic experiences [cannot] be articulated'. She also indicates that they have to be 'repressed' (1984: 52), although Goldberg would see this as vertical (disavowal) rather than horizontal (repression) splitting. An equally important effect is that generative and creative gestures are not cultivated or supported either. The literature on creativity describes a period of gestation or incubation during which creative artistic expression or new scientific insights slowly take shape (see Example 6 in Chapter 1, p. 8). Citing biographical accounts of this creative process, Stern (1997: 95) comments: 'The unformulated must organize itself first. It must begin to coalesce . . . [to] send out tendrils, or feelings of tendency.'

The nurturing of 'feelings of tendency' is an important aspect of the work of therapy. The therapist does not pretend to know how clients should live, how their unique constellation of capacities and interests should take shape in the unfolding of the rest of their life. Therapy not only involves the emerging into formulation of past experience. The idea of a buried true self implies that therapists also support and witness the emerging into formulation of a new way of being. For this to happen, both client and therapist need a stance of openness, curiosity and acceptance of uncertainty, and therapists need to develop the 'ability to see as yet unrealized possibilities' in their clients and an 'openness to new and unforseen ways of relating to [them]' (Summers 1999: 110).

Prereflective, dynamic and unvalidated

Although they present the prereflective, dynamic and unvalidated as distinct 'realms' of the unconscious, Stolorow and Atwood point out that in practice they interpenetrate each other. Often material is unconscious in both unvalidated and dynamic senses, in that it is both walled off because it is associated with emotional conflict and not articulated because it has not received validating responses from others. Stern (1997: 81) captures the two aspects together in the elegant phrase 'defensively motivated unformulated experience'.

This interpenetration can be seen in Bollas's work with the earliest relational schemas, which lay the foundation for future personality development. At this stage Bollas (1987: 13) refers to the mother as a 'transformational object' because her presence is the source of a succession of different ego states that continuously transform the infant's sense of itself. These primitive schemas are prelinguistic: 'we learn the grammar of our being', writes Bollas (1987: 36), 'before we grasp the rules of our language'. Within the normal discourses of everyday life, therefore, experiences that are rooted in disturbed early self–object schemas are difficult to acknowledge. This is the territory of the 'unthought known'. By seeing clients five days a week, and cultivating a meditative, receptive state, Bollas enables clients to re-experience these early relational modes. Through feeling within himself the bodily and emotional quality of the client's regressed state, he attempts to 'somatically register' (1987: 282) the client's relational world. In due course, he is ready to formulate in words what has until now 'been buried as a deep structure' (1987: 9) and remained 'more an operational and less a representational form of knowledge' (1987: 281). By giving them 'a certain dosage of time, space and attentiveness in which to emerge' (1987: 278), Bollas allows these states to be experienced in a context within which they can be acknowledged and formulated for the first time. This provides clients with a crucial step towards integrating what happened to them into the broader narrative of their life and world.

Bollas describes the 'unthought known' as 'the unrepressed unconscious' (1987: 70). It is unconscious in the prereflective sense, since these 'complex rules for being and relating' (1987: 9) constitute the organizing principles that shape experience. It is also unconscious in the unvalidated sense, since it includes 'those experiences in a child's life which were simply beyond comprehension' (1987: 246). Bollas's framework also includes the 'primary repressed unconscious': painful states of relationship with the mother from birth and even *in utero* which could not be integrated into later development. This is material that is unconscious in the dynamic sense.

The absolute and relative unconscious

Since the process of formulating unformulated experience takes place in a social context, what Freud called repression and conceptualized intrapsychically can be reconceptualized as an interpersonal process. In everyday conversation, what is spoken about, how it is spoken about and the way matters are broached or avoided is continuously orchestrated in response to subtle social cues, which enforce a complex system of unspoken rules of discourse. In conversation analysis, the influence of this hidden rule system can be detected in virtually every utterance. Billig (1999: 52) suggests that in this way conversation effectively creates the unconscious:

> to say one thing implies that other things are not being said. If language provides the rhetorical skills for opening up lines of talk, then it also provides the skills for creating the unsaid. More than this, language provides the skills for closing down areas of talk.

This approach invites us to consider how the conversation between client and therapist might be understood to undo the unconscious. Fourcher (1992: 320, 321) suggests two approaches. On the one hand, there is the reflective task of 'explicating what is implicit in experience'. This suggests the metaphor of a lens, which brings into focus what was formerly only vague and unformulated. Therapy is, in effect, an extension of normal conversational practices to areas of life that are often neglected; it addresses the 'relative unconscious', a phrase initially used by Ricoeur. By contrast, there are the areas of talk that, from Billig's perspective, clients expect would be rapidly shut down were they to broach them. In classical psychoanalysis, these areas are believed to underlie the client's symptoms and are kept unconscious by defences and resistances. These are addressed by the therapist's active attempts to influence and persuade, in order to instigate the 'uncovering' or 'shaking loose' of the impacted material.

This suggests another metaphor, of a shovel. Fourcher (1992: 324) uses the term 'absolute unconscious' for this kind of material, which represents 'the formal otherness of human self-alienation'.

Therapists who favour the lens metaphor focus on the relative unconscious and conceptualize therapy in terms of formulation of experience and construction of narratives. Those who are drawn to the shovel metaphor focus on the absolute unconscious and conceptualize therapy in terms of finding and unearthing what is alienated and repressed. Fourcher suggests we need a framework that bridges the two. It is easy to idealize the social process of the construction of experience into a narrative that is consensually validated. But this assumes a reciprocity and symmetry in the experiences of those engaged in the process. In practice, however, people frequently fail to understand each other perfectly. Consequently, 'alongside a unified linguistic consciousness' (1992: 327), we inevitably find heterogenous individual experience that remains unintegrated, unvalidated and 'structurally distinct'. Fourcher suggests, therefore, that therapists need to be aware of and reflect on the different ways they participate in the 'social dialectic' of the therapy relationship, and recognize how they shift between a more lens-like stance on some occasions, and a more shovel-like approach on others.

Unconscious communication

We see this kind of relational perspective at its most radical in Langs's communicative psychotherapy, which is based on the concept of unconscious communication between client and therapist. This extends Ferenczi's (1915: 109) concept of 'dialogues of the unconscious', in which 'the unconscious of two people completely understand themselves and each other, without the remotest conception of this on the part of the consciousness of either'. In the course of evolution, Langs argues, humans came to the fore through their capacity to work cooperatively in a group. In order to safeguard this cooperativeness, a 'deep unconscious wisdom system' (Langs 1996: 171) evolved, which could automatically monitor the honesty and genuineness of the affective engagement of others and respond to regulate it when others are perceived to be dishonest. This regulation is achieved through the sharing of narratives. By telling each other stories, individuals communicate their feelings to other group members in an indirect way.

This system is in action in the therapy situation, which is inevitably characterized by a power struggle, often unacknowledged, between client and therapist (Langs 1983; Holmes 1999; Smith 1999a, 1999b; see Example 9 in Chapter 1, p. 12 for the effects of unrecognized power differentials). Although therapists are paid to help the client, their unconscious motives for becoming therapists may interfere with their ability to do this. For example, they may have become therapists because of a need to feel in control of their own unwanted impulses, or because of a fascination with the private details of others' lives, or for the self-esteem they gain from being a good caring helper. It is easy for a discourse of resistance and defences (Fourcher's shovel) to structure the relationship in a way that enables therapists to maintain power over the client and hide their own vulnerabilities. Whenever there is a difference of opinion, the therapist can attribute the client's perspective to resistance or defence. This has led to the quip that 'psychoanalysis is the only business where the customer is always wrong' (Holmes 1999: 41).

A relational perspective recognizes that just as the therapist provides a mirror for the client, so, inevitably, the client holds up a mirror for the therapist (Smith 1999b). Ferenczi (1933: 293) suggested, much to the alarm of Freud and his followers, that clients indirectly convey 'repressed or suppressed criticisms' of the therapist. Communicative therapists take this idea seriously. A client complained that her mother never answered the telephone, and added, 'She just doesn't make an effort.' The communicative therapist might 'decode' the unconscious communication as follows: in speaking of feeling neglected by someone who is not making an effort, the client is conveying that right now she is feeling neglected by the therapist; perhaps this is because she has been sitting passively for most of the session and has not been adequately meeting her client's needs. What the therapist actually did was to attempt to confront the client with her own passivity: 'You might really be angry with yourself for not getting on with your life.' The client responded by explaining that if she tried to speak reasonably, her mother would put the blame on her; and added, 'It isn't fair . . . she always wants to avoid responsibility.' The communicative therapist would 'decode' this as meaning: 'You, therapist, have really been unresponsive to my attempts to be in touch with you . . . When I express this . . . you respond aggressively, blaming my feelings on me . . . you are not pulling your weight in this relationship' (Smith 1999a: 6–7).

Relational therapists recognize that they cannot stand outside the interaction with the client as if they were a neutral party. Instead, 'the unconscious is lived out, negotiated, and constructed' within the matrix of therapist's and client's ever shifting experiences of each other (Hirsch and Roth 1995: 268). For communicative therapists, this means that to respond in a manner that addresses their clients' concerns in a genuine way, they must use clients' unconscious communications as a means to identify 'their own errors in the consulting room . . . to confess these mistakes to the [client] and to modify them in response to the [client's] unconscious suggestions' (Holmes 1999: 40). It is perhaps not surprising that this recommendation evokes considerable resistance from many therapists, perhaps because it means 'acting in contradiction to our evolved talent for remaining unaware of our own exploitativeness' (Smith 1999b: 32).

Conclusion

Despite the almost complete abandonment of Freud's classic models of unconscious processes, one way in which the historical debt to Freud continues to be acknowledged is through the language of the unconscious. As Hirsch and Roth (1995: 263) observe, 'inherent in anything called psychoanalysis is some notion of unconscious processes'. But 'the unconscious' is no longer employed as a propositional explanatory construct in the way it was in Freud's topographical model. In many major works on object relations theory, 'the unconscious' or even 'unconscious' as an adjective are hardly used, and we find no reference to them at all in the index. Often where there is an entry, the terms only appear in the presentation of Freud's classical theories. This does not imply that unconscious factors are not considered important. On the contrary, their influence is taken for granted. However, when 'the unconscious' or 'unconscious processes' are referred to, this happens in such a variety of ways that Hirsch and Roth (1995: 263) even remark that 'it has become unclear what we mean when we talk about unconscious experience'. We find a similarly fluid situation among cognitive-behaviour therapists. They have not traditionally been associated with an interest in unconscious processes. But, as we will see in Chapter 6, it is not as simple as that.

CHAPTER 6

Cognitive therapy, cognitive science and the cognitive unconscious

The once fashionable skeptical position of many academic psychologists – that empirical findings do not warrant belief in psychologically significant unconscious cognitive phenomena – has crumbled in the face of recent research.

(Greenwald 1992: 773)

The real work in navigating through the problem spaces of our lives is done unconsciously for most of us most of the time . . . We have a vast unconscious domain and we gain access to it by using consciousness . . . The big puzzle is, why is the conscious aspect so limited, and the unconscious part so vast?

(Baars 1997: 294, 297, 304)

From behaviour therapy to cognitive-behaviour therapy

Behavioural and cognitive therapists have always been concerned to interface their theories with the findings of experimental research, and have, therefore, been particularly influenced by the dominant ideological positions within academic psychology. During the course of the twentieth century these underwent considerable changes. A century ago, as we saw in Chapter 2, psychologists artificially separated out consciousness from its broader context. The introspectionist methodology that this approach relied on eventually proved limited and sterile and the behaviourist reaction against it diminished the importance of consciousness altogether. Behaviourists assumed that the question of the relationship between mind and body could be solved by equating consciousness with certain kinds of brain process, and some expected that, once science had advanced far enough, the language of consciousness and psychological states would be superseded by rigorous scientific description of nervous system activity.

Although not denying the existence of conscious awareness, behaviourists believed that a science of behaviour could proceed with little or no reference to it. Skinner's (1953) programme for psychology was the development of a functional analysis of the relationships between environmental variables and behaviour. He placed inverted commas round ordinary language terms that refer to 'thought processes' or to the manner in which the solution to a mathematician's problem unexpectedly 'pops into his [*sic*] head', arguing that they need to be rephrased in a manner that 'removes much of the mystery that surrounds these terms'. Instead of speaking of how the mathematician had 'continued to work on the problem "unconsciously"', Skinner preferred to say that, with the passage of time, changes occurred in the variables that controlled the response: 'Variables which have interfered with a solution may grow weak, and supporting variables may turn up' (Skinner 1953: 252).

There were several useful clinical applications of behavioural technology. In systematic desensitization, clients were trained in relaxation. They would then have sessions in which they visualized a feared object (such as a snake or spider) or situation (giving a speech in public) and relaxed themselves as soon as the anxiety became uncomfortable. This procedure was successful in addressing many phobias. Contingency management was applied effectively to eliminate disruptive behaviour and train new adaptive behaviour in children in the classroom and at home and in residents in psychiatric hospitals. The principles were also used to toilet train individuals with severe mental retardation, some of whom had been incontinent for decades (Wolpe *et al.* 1964; Craighead *et al.* 1976).

Behaviour therapists spoke about these processes in the language of laboratory research in conditioning, and attempted to discredit therapists with other approaches who had 'not yet mastered or endorsed the jargon of respondents, operants and reinforcements' (London 1972: 913). They firmly rejected concepts, such as 'the unconscious' or even 'unconscious processes', that were associated with psychoanalysis. This ideological conflict obscured the fact that unconscious processes were exactly what their powerful new technology was addressing. Behaviour therapy was built on the recognition that much behaviour is habitual and automatic and that individuals have only limited awareness of the sources and the details of their own behaviour, motivations and emotions. Skinner observed how people are often unaware of how aggressive they appear to others or of their own facial expressions, and even referred to 'unconscious mannerisms' without using inverted commas (Skinner 1953: 289). He used the phrase 'absence of self-knowledge' (1953: 288) to refer to psychological processes that take place out of awareness, such as the processes that lead to the sudden emergence of a solution to a mathematical problem. He conceived of self-knowledge as 'a special repertoire' of covert behaviour that would vary in extent depending on an individual's learning history, and that would inevitably be very limited in scope.

Behaviour therapists demonstrated that significant changes in behaviour could be brought about without relying on introspection and conscious reflection on the part of the client. Unfortunately, this important lesson was lost on many therapists from other orientations because, by turning their backs on the language of thoughts, beliefs, expectations and intentions, behaviourists communicated in a discourse that many found alienating and that imposed another kind of sterility on the discipline.

Cognitive therapy: focus on strategic processes

By the 1960s it was clear that a coherent and accessible psychology could not be developed without reference to cognitive factors. Skinner's own demonstrations of the effects of reinforcement schedules showed that behaviour is not simply predictable on the basis of immediate 'contextual variables', but is influenced by past experience; this, of course, is represented by means of abstractive and constructive cognitive process. It was simply cumbersome and limiting to speak of psychological and behavioural problems without referring to cognitive factors. The 'cognitive revolution' redirected attention to those thoughts and images which are available to intro-spection, and these were seen as playing a complementary role along-side the conditioning processes the behaviourists had charted. This dual focus on the behavioural technology of operant and classical conditioning on the one hand, and work with accessible cognitive processes on the other, was to consolidate into the contemporary distinction between automatic and strategic processes. Automatic processes are rapid, effortless, involuntary, unintentional, operate entirely or largely outside of conscious awareness and consume minimal attentional capacity; strategic processes are voluntary, intentional, effortful, relatively slow, conscious and consume attention (Brewin 1988; McNally 1995; Beck and Clark 1997; Bargh and Chartrand 1999; Kihlstrom 1999). The therapy that put the two together was named cognitive-behaviour therapy, a term that carried clear connotations of the divide between conscious and unconscious: the 'behaviour' part pointed to automatic (unconscious) processes and the 'cognitive' part to strategic (conscious) ones. The first cognitive interventions, therefore, focused on processes that are available to consciousness.

Therapists were also concerned to extend clients' awareness of their automatic behaviours, and employed a range of self-monitoring exercises to achieve this. As Alford and Beck (1997: 125) remark, 'cognitive therapy aims to make conscious certain processes that were initially unconscious'. Anxious clients are asked to notice physiological responses such as feelings of heat, choking, elevated heart rate and muscular tension. Attention is also paid to automatic thoughts such as 'I can't cope with this' or 'They'll laugh at me', and to automatic images, such as of oneself collapsing on the ground or of people jeering. Many clients begin treatment with little awareness of their differing emotional states. Through self-monitoring and psychoeducation, they can learn to discriminate and accurately name basic emotions. Behavioural monitoring increases awareness of the frequency of problematic habits such as tobacco or alcohol consumption, hair pulling or skin-picking, or of the details of everyday eating patterns or work or leisure activities.

Other methods are also employed to increase awareness of automatic behaviour. Specific contexts may be set up in which therapists can monitor clients' behaviour and provide feedback. Socially anxious clients may role-play problematic interpersonal situations, and therapists can draw attention to avoidance of eye contact, speech hesitations, difficulties with fluent breathing and other behaviours relevant to skilled social interaction. Role-plays can be videotaped so that therapists can watch the interaction process with their clients and point out particular behaviours. The deliberate extension of everyday awareness is, therefore, a central feature of the cognitive-behavioural approach.

As clients become aware of problematic aspects of experience and behaviour, they can learn to interrupt and change them. As Adler observed (see Chapter 3, p. 40), sometimes this occurs spontaneously: simply recognizing a self-defeating habit is enough to set in motion whatever is needed to change it (Mahoney and Thoresen 1974).

However, generally it calls for the application of strategic activity aimed at the intentional regulation of behaviour. Socially anxious individuals can learn new conversational skills, or be trained to pause between sentences and take regular breaths while making a speech, so as to avoid running out of breath and feeling dizzy. Panicky patients can be taught to pace their breathing and breathe shallowly, as a means of preventing hyperventilation and the uncomfortable physical symptoms that it produces (Clark 1997).

Another important set of strategic processes focuses on working directly with thoughts and images. In self-instructional training, for example, clients practise inner speech, which guides them through a stressful situation in an adaptive manner (e.g. 'no need to panic, I know how to do this, keep focused on what I have to say'). Self-critical thinking plays a role in maintaining many cases of depression, and in such cases, training in self-reinforcement and accurate self-evaluation can help to break the depressive cycle ('Well done, I expressed myself clearly and she seemed to be genuinely interested in what I said'). A range of metacognitive processes involve acting directly on thoughts and images: distraction can help reduce the intensity of anxiety ('let me focus on the clothes people are wearing, rather than on my anxiety symptoms') or thought stopping can reduce the frequency of intrusive thoughts and images that are disturbing. Most importantly, negative thinking that contributes to dysfunctional emotions and behaviour can be addressed through rational evaluation and responding. For example, a young man who is giving a lecture might think, 'They are looking to see if I make a mistake so that they can laugh at me.' However, with training he can learn to remind himself, 'They are more likely to be focusing on the content of what I am saying as they have to write a test next week.' Therapeutic interventions involving training of these kinds of consciously controlled strategic processes began to be applied to a wide range of clinical presentations, including depression, anxiety, problems with impulse control and even psychotic disorders. Case reports and treatment trials have demonstrated their effectiveness in treating depression, phobias, panic attacks, social anxiety and bulimia in significant numbers of clients. There are also successful applications in improving the impulse control in clients whose difficulties stem from their aggressiveness or illegal sexual behaviour (Wilson and O'Leary 1980; Masters *et al.* 1987; Salkovskis 1996; Clark and Fairburn 1997; Spiegler and Guevremont 1998).

Spurred on by the successes gained from focusing on strategic processes, clinical theorists began to reconceptualize many interventions that had initially been understood in terms of conditioning. Systematic desensitization, originally explained by Wolpe as a process of counter-conditioning, was reframed as a training in self-awareness and self-regulation (Mahoney and Thoresen 1974); and a cognitive factor – self-efficacy (the client's belief that she or he can handle what was previously a threatening situation) – was shown to be a critical variable in predicting its effectiveness (Bandura 1997). Many took the view that it would soon be possible to develop briefer and briefer treatments, and to offer significant help to a larger proportion of clients. There seemed to be no limits to what conscious self-regulation could achieve, and the project of bringing more and more problematic behaviours under conscious control was seen to depend on the ingenuity of therapists in the development of new strategic techniques and the hard work of clients in applying them. This development merely entrenched behaviourists' suspicion of psychodynamic constructs. In his influential social-cognitive theory, Bandura (1986: 3) criticizes explanations for behaviour that invoke the 'inner dynamics of unconscious mental functions'; and Wilson and O'Leary (1980: 280) observe that cognitive-behaviour therapists are primarily concerned 'with conscious thought processes, rather than unconscious symbolic meanings . . . It is unnecessary to determine the unconscious roots of irrational or inaccurate interpretations of reality.'

The limits of strategic, directed awareness

But there were limitations to this approach. Many clients lacked the motivation actively to help themselves, others could not identify significant patterns of thought linked to their problems and in others, irrational thoughts and assumptions were not easy to shift by cognitive restructuring (McGinn and Young 1996; Power 1997). It became clear that many of the personal meanings that are central to understanding why people feel and behave as they do are not in the form of thoughts or images that are immediately available to awareness. The new faith in strategic interventions was a return to the heroic view of consciousness that preceded Freud, and heralded a new ideological struggle around the relationship between conscious and unconscious processes.

Some, like Albert Ellis, minimize the difficulties involved. Although he refers to the 'conscious and unconscious evaluations, interpretations and philosophies' (Ellis 1973: 56) that underlie emotional responses to everyday situations, he states with his accustomed crispness:

> no part of a human being is to be reified into an entity called the unconscious . . . 'unconscious' thoughts and feelings are, for the most part, slightly below the level of consciousness . . . and can usually be brought to consciousness by some brief, incisive probing.
>
> (Ellis 1989: 210–11)

Others recognize that accessing the personal meanings that are related to clients' problems is not always so straightforward. In Aaron Beck's approach to cognitive therapy, three levels of cognition are identified (Greenberg 1997; J. S. Beck 1995). *Automatic thoughts and images* may flash by unnoticed, but they can fairly easily be brought to awareness by questioning and by training clients in self-monitoring. When this happens, clients are often surprised at the variety and range of the stream of negative thinking that they discover. *Underlying assumptions* take the form of rules people live by or expectations that they take for granted (for example, 'I should not get angry with my mother'; or 'if they see what I really feel, they will reject me'; or 'I need to ensure that I have everyone's approval all of the time'). Because they may not be recognized until brought to light in therapy, Beck *et al.* (1979: 80) call them 'silent' assumptions. At the third level of cognition are *core beliefs*, absolute beliefs, usually about the self or other people; for example, 'People can't be trusted', or 'I'm unlovable', or 'I'm different from other people – there's something wrong with me.' These often seem to be part of a person's identity and to be particularly resistant to change.

Thus Hackmann (1997: 125–6) observes that

> focusing on the first thoughts that come up may miss much of the meaning of an upsetting event . . . we need to tackle both the surface weeds (negative automatic thoughts, images etc.) and the deeper 'roots' (underlying beliefs and assumptions) of the meanings we give to events.

Brewin (1988: 173) remarks that this 'is often an extremely difficult process that requires great caution'. It calls for therapist skills in case conceptualization and the sensitive application of specific techniques. A great deal of attention in the cognitive therapy literature is paid to methods that bring to light those meanings that are not easily accessed. Padesky (1996) discusses how she will listen not only to what clients say, but also 'to what they're not saying and try to use this to ask further informational questions so we can begin to look at information that might be out of their current awareness'. The 'vertical arrow' technique (Burns 1990: 124) is widely used to bring to awareness underlying assumptions and core beliefs. Here, the therapist repeatedly asks the client 'What if?':

'If I blow the exam, I may fail the course.'
(What if you fail the course?)
↓

'That would mean I was a failure and people would think less of me.'
(What if people think less of you?)
↓

'Then I'd feel terrible, because I need people's approval to feel happy and worthwhile.'

Clients might be asked to engage in some 'thoughtful reflection' on an upsetting situation (Hackmann 1997: 125), or to visualize it vividly and experience it as if it were happening here and now (Beck and Emery 1985). The underlying meaning of problematic feelings can also be explored with guided imagery (Edwards 1990), or by using Gendlin's (1978, 1996) focusing technique, where clients are asked to focus on their overall bodily 'felt sense' of the problem and allow a word or phrase or image to arise spontaneously.

Here is an example of how a simple technique can bring underlying meanings to awareness: a woman in her late twenties, who very much wanted to find a husband and have a family, mentioned this wish rather indirectly. It took careful questioning to establish that this was one of her central concerns. The therapist commented on her difficulty in owning the problem and asked her to close her eyes and say to herself: 'I want to find a partner and settle down and have a family, and as the months go by this is feeling more and more urgent.' Immediately she remembered being four years old at her grandparents' house, watching them quarrelling bitterly. She also recalled her own parents' quarrels and thought about several friends who had married and quite soon after divorced. All this took her by surprise. She had been unaware that her fears of marital conflict were contributing to her present difficulties.

The cognitive analysis of automatic processes

Meanwhile, important developments were taking place in experimental cognitive research. With the demise of behaviourism, automatic processes were reconceptualized in information-processing terms, and cognitive processes that occurred independently of conscious awareness and control began to be demonstrated in the laboratory. In one study, participants heard random sequences of tones played into one ear. A story was heard in the other ear and participants had to check the spoken story against a written version. Their attention was almost entirely devoted to tracking the story so that there was little or no processing of the tone sequences: on a recognition test of tone sequences they had heard five times, they scored just above the chance level. However, when they were asked to say how much they liked the tones, they liked sequences they had heard before better than new ones. Prior exposure to the sequences resulted in a 'differential affective reaction' to them, even though they did not recognize them and they did not sound familiar (Zajonc 1980: 162).

The term 'implicit memory' is now used for these situations in which a prior experience that a person does not explicitly recognize or recall exercises an influence on subsequent behaviour. 'Priming' is another implicit memory effect. For example, participants see a series of words with several missing letters (e.g. RAB – – –) and are asked to identify the whole word (RABBIT). They can do this more quickly if they have read the whole word (the prime) some while before. The effect occurs even if participants do not recognize that they have seen the prime before, and is still evident a week after being exposed to it. This is quite different from recognition memory, which degrades considerably in a week (Schacter 1996).

Jacoby *et al.* (1992: 802) describe several experiments which demonstrate that a 'source of influence unavailable to consciousness has an effect on thought and behavior'. They also demonstrate the limitations of strategic processes, using a memory-based illusion effect. In one experiment participants listened to sentences against a background of white noise. Some were new sentences and others they had heard before. The background noise sounded quieter for familiar sentences than for new ones. Participants were explicitly told about the effect and asked to try to avoid it; however, they continued to judge the noise as quieter when sentences were familiar. This kind of finding led Baars (1997: 303) to observe: 'We rarely have much access to the reasons why we do anything, and when we are forced to guess we are often wrong.'

Neuropsychological studies of brain-damaged individuals provide further important observations. Weiskrantz (1997) documents the phenomenon of 'blindsight', in which individuals with damage to the occipital cortex can be shown to respond correctly to visual stimuli even though they report no phenomenal experience of them. One research subject could tell whether a circular patch of stripes was oriented horizontally or not or whether a stimulus was moving or stationary: 'In many cases he said he was just guessing, and thought he was not performing better than chance. When he was shown his results . . . he expressed open astonishment' (Weiskrantz 1997: 18). Through studies like these neuropsychologists are now able to show that many brain pathways process a great deal of complex information without any direct conscious experience being associated with them, and that the experience of conscious awareness depends on activity in quite specific sites and pathways in the brain.

Since the research subject's ability to make visual discriminations was 'disconnected from a conscious, acknowledged awareness' (1997: 59) of the fact, he could not make practical use of it. In implicit learning, by contrast, individuals are aware they have learned something and are able to put their learning to practical use, but they are unable to report on what it is they know (Reber 1993). In implicit learning research, participants learn complex new skills, similar in many ways to learning language. In one study, an artificial 'language' was generated using a small number of letters that could occur in strings from three to eight letters long according to fixed rules that generated a total of 43 'grammatical' strings. In each trial, participants were asked to commit four strings to memory, and the number of errors they made before reaching a criterion was noted. A 'grammar' group worked only with grammatical strings. A 'random' group worked with the same letters arranged randomly. At first, both groups made a similar number of errors, but after a while, the 'grammar' group continued to improve and the random group did not. This means they were learning the rules that generated the grammar. When they were shown new sequences, they were able to recognize whether or not they were grammatical. Yet they had not been told that there were underlying rules and that they should learn them. Nor were they consciously aware of the rules, and they could not state them. This is just what we find in young children who can speak grammatical sentences but cannot describe the rules that underlie them. In other studies, participants can be shown to have learned the underlying rules that generate a complex sequence of light flashes even though they are completely unable to describe them. Participants to whom the underlying rules are explained perform no faster than others who are not given this information. Indeed, in some studies participants who can describe some of the underlying regularities perform worse. This is probably because giving attention to strategic processing diverts resources from the processes involved in the automatic, implicit learning.

Implicit learning can thus be defined as 'the acquisition of knowledge that takes place largely independently of conscious attempts to learn and largely in the absence of explicit knowledge of what was acquired' (Reber 1993: 5). It is based on 'deep information about the nature of the structure of a sequence of events' (1993: 47), which is automatically encoded as a cognitive representation of the complex patterns of covariation in the environmental events to which individuals are exposed. It is 'fundamentally inaccessible to ... consciousness because it involves a more advanced and structurally more complex organization than could be handled by consciously controlled thinking' (Lewicki *et al.* 1992: 796). Reber calls this 'tacit knowledge', a term taken from the philosopher Polanyi (1958).

These developments led to a revolution in academic attitudes to unconscious processing. Bowers and Meichenbaum (1984), in *The Unconscious Reconsidered*, examine their implications for our understanding of psychopathology and psychotherapy in general and cognitive-behaviour therapy in particular. Cognitive psychologists even began to be drawn to that culturally familiar phrasing 'the ... unconscious'. One of the contributors to the Bowers and Meichenbaum book published an article in *Science* entitled 'The cognitive unconscious' (Kihlstrom 1984, 1987). Interest in unconscious processes and even 'the unconscious' had found its way back into the heart of the academic establishment! Later, Kihlstrom (1999; Kihlstom *et al.* 2000) would use the terms 'emotional unconscious' and 'motivational unconscious'. The term 'cognitive unconscious' had been introduced by Rozin (1979: 256) to refer to highly specialized 'tightly wired' information processing systems that are not accessible to introspection or strategic control. An example is the system whereby bees find their way to food using the position of the sun and automatically correct for its movement across the sky. Another is the pre-attentive perceptual system, which calculates the size and distance of objects using cues such as the degree of convergence of the eyes, the disparity of the two images on the retina, gradients of texture, the occlusion of one object by another and the height of an object in the field. Helmholtz had, of course, referred to the 'unconscious inference' involved here over a century earlier (see Chapter 2, p. 22). These kinds of abilities are mediated by highly specialized systems in the brain, which are the product of a long evolutionary history, much of which took place millions of years ago at a time when strategic processes played a much more limited role in the management of behaviour.

Defining the relationship between automatic and strategic processes

The cognitive unconscious appears to manage baseline automatic activities, while conscious cognition is part of the strategic processing that deals with more complex and challenging matters. However, this dichotomous categorization can be simplistic and misleading, since four different concepts, which do not entirely overlap, have been drawn on in making the distinction between the two domains. First, the distinction can be made on the basis of whether a process is available to awareness. Processes that are 'unconscious in the strict sense that they are inaccessible to phenomenal awareness under any circumstances' (Kihlstrom 1999: 426) are clearly automatic and part of the cognitive unconscious. Second, the distinction can be made on the basis of attentional capacity. Attention can be focused on only a small part of the information that is currently available and the systems that underlie strategic processes depend on this limited capacity. Automatic processes, by contrast, are not limited in the same way. In terms of contemporary models of information processing, strategic processes compete for access to a central processing unit with a limited capacity, while automatic processes occur in systems that operate separately and in parallel (Greenwald 1992; McNally 1995; Kihlstrohm 1999). In practice, there is some overlap between this concept and that of being available to awareness, since reporting awareness of a stimulus takes attentional capacity. However, in some experimental situations it is easier to show that an activity uses some of the available capacity than to show that it is registered in awareness. Third, the distinction can be made on the basis that automatic processes are involuntary and strategic ones are voluntary (McNally 1995; Kihlstrohm 1999). Finally, the term 'unconscious' is used to refer to cognitive processes that individuals are unable to report on verbally (Greenwald 1992). This is one of the senses in which Freud used the term when he originally defined repression (Chapter 3, p. 33), and a great deal of debate within psychoanalytic theory has centred on the verbal formulation of experience (Chapter 5, pp. 77–80).

Some processes are clearly unconscious and automatic in all these senses. Pre-attentive perceptual processing, for example, is not available to awareness, appears to consume no capacity, is involuntary and cannot be verbalized. Implicit learning, on the other hand, is automatic and unconscious according to some of these criteria but not others. It is involuntary in that recognition of the underlying rules and regularities occurs in the absence of any intention to learn them. It cannot be reported on verbally in that 'there is an absence of explicit knowledge of what was acquired' (Reber 1993: 5). However, it does consume *some* attentional capacity: individuals must attend to the material about which the learning is to occur, even though they do not attend to the learning process itself. As Baars (1997: 304) neatly puts it, 'Learning just requires us to point our consciousness at some material we want to learn, like some giant biological camera, and the detailed analysis and storage of the material will take place unconsciously.' Because we have to 'point our consciousness' at the material for implicit learning to occur, some critics have argued that it is not truly an unconscious process (Kihlstrom 1999). However, there is a notable absence of strategic processes such as self-instruction, intentional attempts to extract rules or reflection on meaning.

Integrating cognitive science into clinical models

In practice, many of the interventions used by behaviour therapists were quite pragmatic in nature and owed little to experimental laboratory research (London 1972). In the same way, cognitive-behaviour therapy evolved in the clinical setting relatively independently of developments in cognitive science (Stein 1997). Nevertheless, there is an ongoing dialogue between clinical theorists and cognitive scientists, and the developments we have discussed have brought about a deepened respect among cognitive-behaviour therapists for the pervasiveness of unconscious processes, and the difficulties involved in understanding them.

An evolutionary, phylogenetic perspective has been especially important for understanding the processes that underlie fear and anxiety, where a large role is played by 'primal mechanisms', which are 'programmed and largely automatic' (Beck and Emery 1985: 48, 111). These have survival value, especially in early childhood, but in adulthood they can interfere with the operation of the mature cognitive structures that enable individuals to reason effectively. Recent research has shown why these systems are so difficult to work with in psychotherapy. The mechanisms that organize escape or avoidance behaviour are controlled by a 'fear module' in the amygdala (a nucleus of cells situated within the temporal lobe). This can be activated by events that are not consciously registered. This is shown by studies using backward masking, in which a stimulus is briefly presented, followed by another one that prevents the first stimulus from reaching the threshold of awareness. Furthermore, the module is 'encapsulated' and fairly independent of other processes, so it is 'relatively impenetrable to conscious influences' (Öhman and Mineka 2001: 485). Conscious beliefs and attitudes are influenced by activity in the fear module, but this influence does not extend in the other direction. Since the meanings encoded in these tacit 'fear structure[s] . . . can exist in the absence of conscious knowledge of them' (Foa and Kozak 1986: 21), therapists dealing with clients presenting with anxiety may well find that they cannot identify the critical cognitions by relying on 'discussion with the patient' (1986: 28). Even where the underlying meanings are identified, they cannot be restructured through reasoned discussion. The only means by which change can occur is behavioural exposure to the feared situation. This activates the fear module and presents it with corrective information in a manner that allows the fear-laden meanings to be changed. After undergoing a successful exposure intervention, the fear structure no longer encodes the phobic object as dangerous. Once thinking of the phobic object no longer elicits fear, there is also a shift in the client's conscious belief that the object is dangerous.

An ontogenetic perspective has drawn attention to two important aspects of cognitive development. First, there is the gradual development of strategic processes through childhood and adolescence (at birth, of course, behaviour is completely managed by automatic processes). Many strategic cognitive interventions with adults rely on the cognitive systems that underlie abstract reasoning and rational thought. These are products of Piaget's stage of formal operations that are not available until early adolescence. Cognitive restructuring techniques used with adults therefore need to be adapted in working with children (Ronen 1997). However, by age three children can already guide their own behaviour by spoken self-instruction, and in due course this self-instruction takes place covertly. Self-instructional training involves explicitly teaching such skills to those individuals (adults and children) who have failed to develop them at all, or who have learned self-instructions that are dysfunctional and self-defeating (Meichenbaum 1977).

Further, it is recognized that many of the schemas that encode personal meanings that underlie clinical problems date back to infancy and childhood. These cognitive structures are governed by the principles of implicit learning and operate largely independently of conscious strategic processing. In his cognitive reconceptualization of psychoanalytic thinking, Bowlby (1979: 117) drew on the language of information processing and called these schemas 'working models' that represent 'principal features of the world . . . and of [oneself] as an agent in it. [They] determine . . . expectations and forecasts and provide . . . tools for constructing plans of action.' Bowlby examined how these working models encode the child's experience of attachment with the mother or primary caretaker, and incorporate the emotions related to the child's needs and desires and to the consequences of the satisfaction, disappointment or frustration of those needs and desires. This perspective converges with contemporary object relations theory (see Chapter 5) and presents 'the unconscious [as] not so much a seething cauldron of irrationality as an understandable patterning of cognition and affect that has developed from the past and that structures current experience' (Stein and Young 1997: 162). Guidano and Liotti's (1983) influential integration of Bowlby's ideas with Piaget's developmental theory and Beck's cognitive therapy laid the foundation for a cognitive developmental approach to therapy (Leahy 1996; Hackmann 1997) within which the examination of these kinds of tacit knowledge structures is discussed in terms of investigating underlying schemas (Goldfried 1995).

Core beliefs in particular often have their origins in tacit structures laid down in early childhood or infancy. Shirk and Harter (1996: 192) describe the treatment of a depressed 16-year-old boy whose self-critical and perfectionist behaviour was driven by the assumption 'if I am not perfect, I will be rejected'. This was in turn based on the core belief 'something must be wrong with me'. During therapy it became clear that this probably dated back to the age of three months, when his teenage mother had given him up for adoption. He had dealt with the pain of this abandonment by concluding, 'if I had been flawless (perfect), she would have kept me'. Early maladaptive schemas (EMSs) are the focus of Young's schema-focused therapy (Young 1994; McGinn *et al.* 1995; McGinn and Young 1996; Young and Flanagan 1998). These are systems for the organization of the information about self, others and the world that, like the working models described by Bowlby, has its origin in childhood. Young argues that where clients do not respond to brief strategic treatment, the target of change often needs to be the meanings embedded in these schemas.

Childhood schemas are often associated with intense emotional states: Greenberg and Safran (1984) refer to 'emotional schemas' and Teasdale (1996: 32) to 'emotion-related schematic models'. In Young's theory, for example, feelings of emptiness or loneliness accompany the activation of an *emotional deprivation* EMS, while shame and humiliation accompany the activation of a *defectiveness/ shame* EMS. 'Schema control' mechanisms protect individuals from experiencing these intensely painful emotions (Stein and Young 1997: see also Greenberg and Safran 1984); very often it is these control mechanisms that create the problems that bring a person to therapy. For example, schema avoidance involves both behavioural avoidance (avoiding entering situations that might activate the EMS) and cognitive avoidance (avoiding or suppressing images, thoughts or memories about situations, people or events that are thematically related to the EMS). To avoid activating a defectiveness/shame schema, individuals may avoid intimate relationships. As a result they may become lonely and depressed. According to Young, a strategic therapy based on social skills training may fail to address the core sense of defectiveness and the associated shame. Unless the EMS itself is addressed, significant change cannot occur. Many theorists use the term 'emotional processing' when discussing the process of activating and effecting change in these tacit knowledge structures (Foa and Kozak 1986; Safran and Greenberg 1987; Cloitre 1992).

Schema compensation is another schema control mechanism. When things go wrong, individuals with a defectiveness/shame schema may blame other people, or work extra hard to achieve success and the admiration of others. As long as the compensation works, the underlying shame is never experienced. Clients with a dependence/incompetence schema, who feel helpless and unable to cope on their own, may compensate by behaving in an excessively independent manner and never show vulnerability to others. The compensation presents a picture that is often the direct opposite of what is encoded in the underlying EMS. This makes the tacit meanings in the EMS difficult to detect. Only when the compensation fails in some way does the underlying schema become accessible. Schema-focused cognitive therapy employs experiential techniques to activate the EMS that is being avoided or compensated for and to bring the underlying meanings to awareness. These can include using imagery to revisit childhood experiences, engaging in dramatic dialogues between self and parents or other significant figures, watching movies whose themes coincide with the EMS or simply entering situations that were formerly avoided.

Rapprochement

The second half of the twentieth century saw a remarkable ideological shift in academic psychology's approach to unconscious mental processes. Behaviourism, which was often scathing in its rejection of psychoanalytic concepts, assigned unconscious cognitive processes to a 'black box' beyond the reach of science. Reber, whose work on implicit learning has influenced a number of cognitive theorists, remarks on his own previous 'reluctance to use the term *unconscious* to characterize the phenomena appearing with regularity in the laboratory' (original italics). But, as he puts it, that was 'back in the 1960s' (1993: 9). In 1993, taking his cue from Kihlstrom, he subtitled his book *An Essay on the Cognitive Unconscious*. Many cognitively oriented therapists have appropriated this new language into their discourse, with the result that it is no longer controversial to talk about unconscious processes.

However, there is still ambivalence about using terms associated with psychoanalytic theory. Smucker (1997: 201) clearly feels that reference to the language of Freud strengthens the point he is making by providing some historical continuity and precedent; although he does not use the term 'unconscious', he deliberately alludes to Freud's classic language when he distinguishes between 'primary cognitive processing', which is the mode of implicit structures, and 'secondary cognitive processing', which is the mode of the abstract, rational structures. Dowd is more cautious because of concerns that the use of certain terms may connote allegiance to theoretical perspectives and formulations that he does not want to be associated with. He comments that through its 'incorporation of cognitive tacit schemas . . . cognitive therapy has . . . approached the Freudian notion of the unconscious' (Dowd 2000: 6), but later remarks that the domain of tacit knowledge 'has little or nothing to with the Freudian unconscious' (2000: 215; see also Chapter 1). Kihlstrom (1999: 430), who pioneered the introduction of the terms 'cognitive', 'motivational' and 'emotional unconscious' into the contemporary discourse of cognitive science, seems at times to be surprisingly ungenerous towards Freud, arguing that these developments 'owe nothing whatsoever to Freud'.

Others prefer to speak of 'nonconscious' processes. Wessler and

Hankin-Wessler (1989: 245) refer to 'Personal Rules for Living', which are encoded in 'nonconscious algorithms' and which function as 'implicit guides for affective and behavioural responses to situations'. In using the term 'nonconscious' they follow Lewicki, whose research they cite. There is no effective difference in meaning between 'unconscious' and 'nonconscious' in this context. Despite these subtleties of discourse politics, however, there has clearly been a radical shift among many cognitive scientists and many cognitive-behaviour therapists. Dowd and Courchaine (1996: 163) summarize the position succinctly:

> Throughout its relatively short life, cognitive psychotherapy has gradually shifted from an emphasis on conscious thoughts and images to an increasing focus on underlying cognitive schemata that operate at a tacit or 'unconscious' level.

At the same time, as we saw in Chapter 5, psychoanalytic thought about unconscious processes has undergone considerable revision and there has been a great deal of convergence of perspectives. Contemporary cognitive-behaviour therapists address the same range of phenomena that are covered by Stolorow and Atwood's (1999) reformulation of the concept of the unconscious in terms of the prereflective, dynamic and unvalidated 'realms' (see Chapter 5, pp. 72 *sqq.*). First, there are obvious similarities between work with the prereflective unconscious and cognitive-behavioural work, with its wide range of methods designed to bring to clients' awareness the nature of automatic processes (behaviours, emotions, thoughts, images and motivations), as well as to provide insight into the impact of these processes on themselves and on others. Because of the attention to detail that characterizes some specialized applications of cognitive-behaviour therapy, it offers awareness and insight into some kinds of prereflective material that are not normally addressed in other forms of therapy.

Second, in the emphasis on avoidance and compensatory mechanisms that characterizes cognitive developmental approaches we find an alternative formulation of the domain of the dynamic unconscious. This is particularly marked in schema-focused cognitive therapy, which, as Young and Flanagan (1998: 261) observe, 'combines the theoretical depth often associated with psychoanalytic theory with the more active and directive techniques central to cognitive, behavior and experiential therapies'. Schema-focused cognitive therapy incorporates one of Freud's central ideas: that active psychological processes keep significant aspects of our psychological life out of our awareness as a means of avoiding the stirring of memories or associations that are associated with psychological pain. However, the formulation of this in terms of schema controls is closer to that of Adler's theory of safeguarding tendencies and compensatory mechanisms and to Sullivan's account of security operations than it is to Freud's early theories.

Third, a great deal of cognitive therapy addresses the domain of the unvalidated unconscious. Accurate empathy is seen as central to the therapy process. Unless clients experience the therapist as able to acknowledge difficult and painful experiences that have not found validation outside of the therapy context, they will not be able to form a collaborative and trusting relationship. Cognitive therapists are also concerned to discover the unique personal meanings that individuals invest in their everyday situations. These meanings may be more or less accessible, but when therapists enable clients to identify experiences and cognitions embedded in early schemas, they are often offering them the first validation they have ever received for emotionally distressing experiences that, when they occurred in the past, were ignored or met with hostility or rejection (Guidano and Liotti 1983). In describing the application of imagery work to adult survivors of sexual abuse, Layden *et al.* (1993: 86) point out that although as an adult the client may have come to a balanced perspective on what happened, 'the "child" still remains convinced that the abuse was his [or her] fault, therefore the intervention must attend not only to the adult . . . but [to] the "child" of many years ago'. The first stage of 'attending to the child' is to offer acknowledgement and validation of the original experience.

Thus, despite a tradition of avoiding or de-emphasizing the language of the unconscious and unconscious processes, cognitive-behaviour therapists are no less concerned than therapists of other orientations with the limitations of everyday awareness. Like others, they are also concerned with extending that awareness in various ways. However, as inheritors of the behavioural tradition, they give greater recognition than some other approaches to the well-attested finding that conscious reflection and insight is significantly limited in bringing about changes in tacit knowledge structures, unless they are complemented by active change techniques such as behavioural exposure and behavioural experiments. Broadly speaking, however, what this chapter shows is that, despite some critical posturing on both sides in the past, currently both cognitive and psychoanalytic therapists address similar kinds of unconscious material, even if their methods of doing so and their ways of talking about it still differ.

CHAPTER 7

Invisible worlds, unconscious fields and the non-egoic core: evolving discourses of the transpersonal unconscious

> We are unconscious of our minds. Our minds are not unconscious. Our minds are conscious of us . . . It is only from a remarkable position of alienation that the source of life, the Fountain of Life, is experienced as the It. The mind of which we are unaware is aware of us.
>
> (Laing 1989: 46–7)

The theorists we examine in this chapter follow Jung in believing that the world of everyday experience is founded upon another order of reality that is radically hidden from view, a spiritual matrix that is active and intelligent, that has its own life and process and within which each individual awareness is just a tiny part. The belief that the world of everyday appearances is founded on a hidden domain is so ancient and culturally widespread that it has been called the 'perennial philosophy' (Huxley 1946) and, more recently, the 'perennial psychology' (Wilber 1975). It is expressed in the ancient Chinese concept of the Tao, which 'underlies and nourishes all of the manifestations, the ten thousand things that can be known' (Bolen 1993: 9). We also find it in the thirteenth-century Italian Christian philosopher St Bonaventure (1217–74), who argued that the world discloses itself through three 'eyes': the eye of flesh furnishes the world of the senses, and together with the eye of mind – the processes of thought and reasoning – provides us with our everyday experience of the consensual world. The eye of contemplation discloses another level, the deeper matrix in which we are all embedded, and without which our account of human life cannot be complete (Wilber 1998).

With the exception of Jung (Chapter 3), and to some extent Boss

(Chapter 4), none of the theorists we have examined so far accommodates the transpersonal perspective in their theories. Nevertheless, a significant number of writers on psychotherapy have always recognized the need to take seriously the spiritual dimension of human life. Thirty years ago, Carl Rogers pointed to the failure of existing biological, cognitive or psychodynamic theories to deal with experiences evoked by the practices of humanistic psychotherapy. He identified the need

> to investigate the possibility that there is a lawful reality which is not open to our five senses; a reality in which past, present, and future are intermingled, in which space is not a barrier and time has disappeared.
>
> (Rogers 1973: 386)

This was a growing perception that led to the emergence of transpersonal psychology and transpersonal psychotherapy as a distinct field in the late 1960s (Metzner 1989; Valle 1989; Rowan 1993; Walsh and Vaughan 1993; Boorstein 1995).

Transpersonal discourses, whether within contemporary psychology or the ancient spiritual traditions (Tart 1992), point to the radical limitations of everyday human awareness and the experience of reality it presents to us. They address the question of how awareness can be extended beyond these limitations to encompass aspects of a hidden spiritual matrix within which everything is fundamentally interconnected. Grof (1985: 129) describes experiences in which individuals feel that their 'consciousness has expanded beyond the usual ego boundaries and has transcended the limitations of time and space', and criticizes forms of therapy that are characterized 'by a rigorous isolation of the problem from its broader interpersonal, social and cosmic context' (1985: 153). Similarly, Hillman (1991: 99) rejects 'the familiar notion of psychic reality based on a system of private experiencing subjects and dead public objects'; and Lombardi and Rucker (1998: 47) criticize conceptual formulations within object relations theory 'due to their rootedness in the premise of separate psyches'. However, although transpersonal theories share this common perspective, they differ markedly in the language they use to speak about it. Here, as in so many areas of psychology, we find multiple discourses, some of which draw heavily on the terms 'conscious' and 'unconscious' and others of which do not.

The visible and the invisible world

There is such a radical difference between the world of ordinary experience and the hidden matrix on which it is founded that some writers speak of two worlds, one visible, the other invisible. In her book *Seeing through the Visible World* Singer (1990: 20) points out the paradoxes inherent in this perspective, because 'what is true in one world is not necessarily true in the other, and vice versa'. Shamans, the healers of traditional societies, are often said to live in two worlds (Bührmann 1984). The term 'shaman', derived from the word for healer in the language of a Siberian tribe, is now widely used to refer to traditional healers who are seen by their societies as technological experts in the workings of the invisible world (Walsh 1990). Mutwa, a Zulu healer, writes:

> behind life there is something fantastic . . . things that are just as wonderful – if not more so – than those things that we do see. We . . . delude ourselves . . . that we are masters of our own destiny . . . there are forces guiding us about which we know nothing.
> (Mutwa 1996: 202)

Shamans are familiar with these paradoxes because they experience the boundaries of ordinary reality as fluid, and work with the kinds of communication that to ordinary consciousness are paranormal. It is no surprise to a shaman if he or she dreams about someone with a particular problem, and that person visits in the next few days for a consultation.

Many transpersonal therapists point out parallels between psychotherapy and shamanic practices. In his work as an art therapist, McNiff (1992: 18) sees himself as 'unconsciously participating in the shamanic tradition'. But he also draws on Hillman's archetypal psychology. Like the theorists of Chapter 4, Hillman avoids the concept of the unconscious because he does not want to be associated with conventional psychoanalytic practice. Instead, he draws on an ancient discourse that goes back at least to the Greek philosopher Plato, which speaks of how the individual soul is embedded in the deeper life of the world soul or *anima mundi* (Roszak 1994). This discourse, which the Romantic poets drew on extensively, uses the term 'imagination' for the process that reconnects the individual to the creative possibilities of the deeper order of existence (see Chapter 2). For Hillman (1997: 111), the world of soul is ever-present, interpenetrating the visible, and 'the copresence of visible and invisible sustains life'. The world is not fundamentally constructed from inert matter, but is alive, expressive, 'ensouled', and it is only our limited awareness, conditioned by the strictures of our cultural discourses, that keeps the invisible world remote. Belief that we inhabit a dead mechanical world 'imprisons us in that tight little cell of ego', writes Hillman (1991: 100), and creates an imbalance between the life of the two worlds. This means, writes Moore (1992: 59), citing Sardello, that 'the object of therapeutic treatment is to return imagination to the things that have become only physical', and in this way to restore the balance. For Moore, psychotherapy is 'the care of the soul', a process that is facilitated by 'the application of poetics to everyday life' (1992: xix). When a client brings a problem to a therapist, it is misleading to think that the therapist is there to stand aside and help from a detached distance. Instead, wittingly or unwittingly, therapist and client are engaging together with archetypal struggles that are the struggles of the world soul itself. 'We are all involved in the soul's therapy', remarks McNiff (1992: 40), so when in the course of art therapy disturbing images emerge, 'it is not just "my" pathology that I encounter but the pathology of the [world] soul' (1992: 26).

Unconscious relational fields

Unlike Western practitioners, shamans do not expect their clients to tell them what they are suffering from. African healers often diagnose what is wrong by mapping on to their own bodies the state of the client's bodily energies and then scanning their own body sensations and noting visual images that occur (Thorpe 1982; Bührmann 1984). Spiritual healers in Western cultures describe energy fields within and around the human body, which are normally out of awareness, and are interested in integrating these concepts with Western medicine and psychotherapy (Karagulla 1967; Kunz and Peper 1984a, 1984b; Brennan 1988). Eden (1993: 203) tells how his grandmother, schooled in Celtic shamanic healing, would 'make direct contact with the patient's auric [energy] body and merge with that body to empathetically perceive the patient's emotions and illness and even to temporarily suffer from that illness'. Direct perception of these kinds of fields is commonly reported in altered states of consciousness induced by psychedelic drugs (Grof 1976), and some people seem to have a spontaneous ability to experience and work actively with them.

These kinds of phenomena are often referred to as 'paranormal' and seen as the domain of 'parapsychology', which addresses controversial phenomena such as telepathy (direct mind to mind communication) and clairvoyance (experience of something that will happen in the future). More recently, the term 'anomalous experiences' has become current (Cardeña *et al.* 2000). Within psychoanalysis there have always been theorists who believe that they have encountered paranormal phenomena that can only be explained in terms of telepathy and clairvoyance. Mintz (1983: 70) describes several examples, including an assessment interview during which she felt repeated sharp pains in her stomach, which 'did not seem to *belong* to me'. She referred the client for a medical examination and a stomach ulcer was detected. In Chapter 3 we saw that Freud became sympathetic to the possibility that telepathy could occur. Considering several cases of apparent telepathic communication, some between therapist and client, he concluded that there was a 'strong balance of probability in favour of thought-transference as a fact . . . One is led to the suspicion that this is the original, archaic method of communication between individuals' (Freud 1933: 43, 55). He speculated that psychoanalytic findings might one day interface with findings in physics to explain the phenomenon. More recently, Singer (1990: xvii) made a similar suggestion: 'I cannot help but wonder whether there might someday be a universal field theory of mind as well as of matter and energy.'

Whereas telepathy might be explained in terms of a field that operates within the normal limits of time and space, other phenomena, such as clairvoyance, transcend these limits. As we shall see, many transpersonal theorists believe that the underlying hidden matrix has field properties that are radically different from those of the gravitational or electromagnetic fields of physics. They often cite David Bohm's distinction between the explicate and implicate orders, which draws on the physics of holography (Bohm and Hiley 1983). The explicate order is the world of ordinary experience, which we mostly take to be reality. The implicate order is the deeper matrix on which it depends. Pribram calls it a 'spectral transform domain' whose properties bring us to

the limit of the usefulness of the distinction between the material and the mental . . . Holography has become a window through which we are able to conceptualize a universe totally different from that which characterizes the world of appearances.

(Pribram 1986: 516–18)

These claims seem to challenge the very basis of common sense, rationality and even science itself. There is, therefore, an ideological polarization of attitudes towards them (Mack 1993). Most psychological theories eschew assumptions about invisible energy fields or hidden domains of existence. Parapsychology has often been actively marginalized or discredited (Child 1985). Bem and Honorton (1994: 16) observe humorously that psychologists may well find that if they start to discuss such things with their colleagues 'such talk provokes most of [them] . . . to roll their eyes and gnash their teeth'.

We see this ideological polarization played out in discussion of a number of puzzling phenomena reported by psychotherapists, in which various kinds of unconscious communication occur between client and therapist (and even the therapist's supervisor). As we shall see, these phenomena are quite different from those that form the basis of Langs's concept of unconscious communication discussed in Chapter 5. Here is an example: a female therapist is seeing a male client who is distant and detached and who refers to her in the third person as 'the counsellor'. She begins to have intrusive and disturbing images of being involved in tender, intimate encounters with him. These feelings are uncharacteristic: she is happily married and these kinds of feelings are not evoked by other male clients. In supervision, it seems that she has somehow taken into herself the client's disavowed longing for intimacy and dependency and the accompanying anxiety and shame, all of which the client has defensively excluded behind his detached manner (Ivey 2001). This phenomenon is often called projective identification. This term was introduced by Melanie Klein, but it has come to be widely used outside of Kleinian discourse. What happens is that during or after a therapy session, a therapist experiences an intense emotional state that is unfamiliar, and that on reflection seems to be a disavowed aspect of the client's experience. The client is unaware of the disavowed material; its transmission to the therapist is not an intentional act; without careful reflection or supervision, the therapist may fail to recognize what has happened. (Projective identification is also discussed from the perspective of the therapeutic relationship by Grant and Crawley 2002.)

One explanation for this phenomenon is that clients automatically evoke the problematic response by means of their verbal and non-verbal behaviour. For example, a suspicious, hostile client might evoke dislike, mistrust and irritation. However, this explanation does not fit the example above. Distant, remote individuals typically evoke boredom and the impulse to withdraw from the relationship. Therefore, some writers argue that clients unconsciously set out to induce in the therapist the very feelings that are problematic for them, and are able to achieve this by subtle manipulation of their verbal and non-verbal behaviour (Issacharoff and Hunt 1994; Harris 1998). Several authors regard this explanation as implausible, and offer an explanation in terms of unconscious interpersonal fields. Stein (1995: 72) points out that in physics a field is defined as 'a pattern of energy flow that affects objects in its domain', and believes that many of the phenomena observed in psychotherapy cannot be understood without invoking some kind of field process. He follows Jung (see Chapter 3, p. 47) in believing that there is a literal 'transfer of psychic contents' (1995: 83) from client to therapist, and uses the metaphor of a virus that travels from the client and infects the therapist's psyche. He believes the process is mediated by an 'interactional field'. We have seen that shamans actively seek to promote this kind of process (see also the concept of embodied countertransference in Rowan and Jacobs 2002). Writers unsympathetic to a transpersonal perspective dismiss this idea disdainfully: Harris (1998: 34) sees no need to invoke 'the magical transposition of one state into the psyche of another'; similarly, Issacharoff and Hunt (1994: 603) are quite categorical that the client cannot 'magically shoot the unwanted content out of his [*sic*] head and into another's'.

Rucker and Lombardi (1998: 49) discuss these kinds of puzzling phenomena in terms of a 'shared unconscious field'. They draw on Matte-Blanco's theory of the unconscious, which is explicated in terms of mathematical set theory. Like so many theories in this chapter, this describes two contrasting modes of experience (Lombardi 1998). Most everyday events are experienced in the asymmetrical mode, which presents a world of multiplicity and difference in which there are clear boundaries between objects (including people) and a predictable and fixed structure of time and space, and within which the rules of Aristotelian logic apply. By contrast, the symmetrical mode discloses an underlying unity beneath the diversity of appearances, within which the structure provided by time and space is permeable and malleable. Experiences in this mode may appear paradoxical to everyday consciousness and be difficult to describe in language. For example, individuals can

> experience being one another, that is each experiencing the other momentarily as of the self . . . The boundaries between the psyches of self and other [fall] away and the participants [find] themselves embedded in like subjectivities.
>
> (Lombardi and Rucker 1998: 45)

This theory is invoked to explain the kinds of phenomena described above, as well as two other paradoxical phenomena. The first is what they call the 'unconscious catch' in supervision (Rucker and Lombardi 1998). Here the field extends to the therapist's supervisor: some disavowed aspect of the client's life that is not recognized by the therapist gets carried into the relationship between the therapist and the supervisor, where it is enacted. Searles (1955) refers to this as 'the reflection process', a term that has generally since become changed to 'parallel process'. Lombardi and Rucker (1998: 37) also describe 'parallel dreaming', where therapist and client have similar dreams. For example, Lynn's therapist dreamed as follows. She is in her house, trying to rouse Lynn, who has fainted. She calls an emergency number but it is disconnected. Men are cleaning the carpet with green foam. Lynn's mother is waiting outside. The therapist realizes that they must get out immediately because the mother and the carpet men are trying to kill her and Lynn with the green foam.

At the next session, Lynn reported a dream of her own that had remarkable parallels to the therapist's. She is in her old house, which is covered in lush greenery. Someone is trying to kill her. She runs through the house looking for her therapist and then phones an emergency number but cannot get through. She is highly anxious and realizes she must get out of the house but cannot find the way. As Lynn and her therapist talked about the two dreams a breakthrough occurred in what had been an impasse in the therapy process, in which Lynn had been stuck for several sessions. This is the kind of phenomenon that Jung called synchronicity (see Chapter 3, p. 47). Rucker and Lombardi recognize that, like other transpersonal theories, the world of appearances is a limited construction that tells only part of the story. They suggest that there is a 'related unconscious' (Rucker and Lombardi 1998: 59), which underlies our everyday experience. This, of course, is the basis of the transpersonal orientation; however, although they refer to Bohm, Rucker and Lombardi do not allude directly to transpersonal psychology. They might even be unhappy about being included in this chapter, since they explicitly distance themselves from the discourses of parapsychology and transpersonal psychology when they indicate that they do not wish to refer to these phenomena as 'telepathic' or 'mystical' (1998: 59).

Schwartz-Salant (1995), by contrast, in discussing the concept of an 'interactive field' between client and therapist, situates himself clearly within a Jungian, transpersonal discourse. An interactive field is more than simply an interpersonal field, since it is connected to the deeper transpersonal matrix. Therapists can focus on and directly experience the field, and in so doing can tune into the flow of energy from client to therapist, as well as archetypal images that feed into the field from the collective unconscious. By embracing the 'essential mystery of work with interactive fields' (1995: 32), therapist and client immerse themselves in a unique transformative process that carries them with its own momentum, and that can bring about a spontaneous reconfiguring of the client's problematic psychological structures. This has parallels with the way Jung spoke of therapy as an 'alchemical vessel', a metaphor that depicts the therapeutic situation as a container into which the raw ingredients of the client's experience are placed. The therapeutic process is like the application of heat to the chemicals, for it sets in motion processes that bring about profound changes. Unlike the alchemical vessel, however, the interactive field is no metaphor. For Schwartz-Salant it is a reality that can be directly experienced and worked with.

Stanislav Grof and the realms of the human unconscious

Focusing on the field in this way calls for an alteration of our everyday mode of awareness. This in turn provides access to specialized resources for healing. This idea is at the heart of most shamanic traditions. Mutwa describes how his grandfather trained him in a form of meditation that enabled him to

> draw knowledge from . . . a huge unseen lake somewhere in the spirit world, where all knowledge of the universe – past, present and future – is to be found. Knowledge lives in that lake in the form of little silver fishes . . . You must just ask the lake . . . to provide you with the knowledge that you seek.
>
> (Mutwa 1996: 14)

Shamans learn to enter altered states of consciousness by means of meditation, chanting, drumming, dancing or psychedelic substances. In the altered state, they may connect with a client's energetic field, or deliberately journey to an upper or lower world where they meet helpers in the form of animals or spirits, who may tell them what is wrong with the patient or what needs to be done to effect healing (Doore 1988; Kalweit 1988; Harner 1990; Walsh 1990).

In 1902, William James, who had studied intensive religious practices, and experienced the alteration of consciousness induced by inhaling nitrous oxide, noted that our normal waking consciousness . . . is but one special type of consciousness, while all about it, parted from it by the filmiest of screens, there lie potential forms of consciousness entirely different. We may go through life without suspecting their existence, but apply the requisite stimulus and at a touch they are there in all their completeness . . . How to regard them is the question – for they are so discontinuous with ordinary consciousness.

(James 1902: 94–5)

However, in the decades that followed, mainstream psychology showed limited interest in the area. Interest was rekindled following the discovery of the psychotropic effects of LSD in 1943 (Stafford 1992). It was distributed to the psychiatric community with the invitation to experiment with it. By the early 1960s, many psychologists, psychiatrists and other health professionals had either taken it themselves or administered it to their clients. The term 'psychedelic' ('mind manifesting') soon became current, as it became apparent that material that it could take years of traditional psychotherapy to uncover could quite quickly emerge into consciousness in an LSD session. Masters and Houston's (1966: 3) classic phenomenological study of psychedelic experiences showed how these substances provided ready access to 'the vast, intricate, and awesome regions we call *mind*'. They argued that cognitive psychology's almost exclusive focus on everyday consciousness failed to take account of 'vast territories of the psyche as yet uncharted by Western psychologists' (1966: 15).

This enthusiasm was tempered when the near universal declaration of psychedelic substances as illegal effectively ended their use in psychotherapeutic treatment. However, the transpersonal perspective has been profoundly influenced by theorists like Grof (1976, 1985, 1998), whose understanding is based on several decades of psychotherapeutic work with non-ordinary states of consciousness induced by psychedelics like LSD, or by holotropic breathwork, a method that involves an extended period of voluntary rapid breathing (hyperventilation) to the accompaniment of evocative music. Grof (1985: 25) deliberately uses the term 'non-ordinary states' because he is concerned that 'altered states' could be taken to imply 'distortions or bastardizations of the correct perception of "objective reality"', which means that they can be dismissed as having no meaning or healing value. However, many transpersonal theorists do use the term 'altered states' (e.g. Tart 1972, 1992). Grof followed the progress of several clients through large numbers of psychedelic sessions, which were interspersed with psychoanalytically oriented discussion sessions. He noticed a great deal of thematic continuity in the material of these sessions and concluded that he was seeing

> a successive unfolding of deeper and deeper levels of the unconscious ... patients often had the feeling that they were returning again to a specific experiential area and each time could get deeper into it.
>
> (Grof 1976: 20)

Psychedelic experiences present in a rich and bewildering array. Grof (1985: 131), however, systematically catalogued them into a 'cartography of the unconscious', which is divided into three major sections: (a) the biographical domain relates to the individual's life experiences from birth onwards, and includes all the material that is typically addressed in psychoanalytic psychotherapy; (b) the perinatal domain covers experiences that are developmentally earlier than many psychotherapists recognize, experiences of birth and even from the womb; (c) the transpersonal domain covers experiences that transcend the normal boundaries of time and space. These include: direct perception of energy fields and energy channels within the body; identification with individuals present and past, or even with whole racial groups, with animals, insects and plants, with rocks, mountains and distant planets; experiences of historical events in great detail, some that are well known, others that are obscure; experiences of other times and places that are so vivid that individuals feel as if they have lived before in a previous incarnation; experiences of archetypal and mythical figures of the kind often described in Jung's psychology – it is as if these mythic realms have their own independent existence and individuals can visit and explore them in an altered state just as easily as they can visit another city in ordinary consciousness (see Chapter 1, Example 10, p. 13); finally, states of profound peace, of a sense of being united with a universal mind or of being at the heart of a great silent void, a 'metaphysical vacuum, pregnant with potential for everything there is [that] appears to be the cradle of all being, the ultimate source of existence' (1998: 30).

Grof sometimes refers to the transpersonal realms as 'the super-conscious' (e.g. Grof 1985: 127), a term that originated with Roberto Assagioli (1888–1974), one of the pioneers of transpersonal psychotherapy. Assagioli (1965) named his approach 'psychosynthe-sis' to emphasize its holistic nature, and to contrast it with 'psychoanalysis'. He distinguished between the lower unconscious (largely corresponding to Freud's id), the middle unconscious (Freud's preconscious) and the higher unconscious, or superconscious, which he saw as the source of intuition, creative inspiration, altruistic emotions and spiritual illumination. He thought of these three levels as being embedded within the collective unconscious described by Jung. Although he differentiated between the superconscious and the collective unconscious, Assagioli never clarified the relationship between them. He conceived of the superconscious as a source of exclusively positive, beneficent material, whereas from Jung's collective unconscious, as from Grof's transpersonal dimensions, can emerge experiences that are both positive and negative, demonic and divine. In fact, Grof (1985: 194) criticizes Assagioli for his 'one-sided emphasis on the light, problem-free, joyful side of life'.

Like other transpersonal theorists, Grof (1998) recognizes two distinctive modes of consciousness. The hylotropic mode provides our everyday experience of the visible world. In this mode, 'we are not really whole, we are fragmented and identify with only a fraction of who we really are' (1998: 5). The holotropic mode provides experiences of non-ordinary states of consciousness, which open up the entire range of the *Realms of the Human Unconscious* (his 1976 book) and disclose the fundamentally spiritual nature of existence:

> The psyche in each of us is essentially commensurate with all existence and ultimately identical with the cosmic creative principle itself . . . spirituality is affirmed as . . . a critical dimension of the human psyche and of the universal scheme of things.
>
> (Grof 1998: 3)

For Grof (1985: 347), like Hillman, psychopathology results from a 'fundamental imbalance between these complementary aspects of human nature'. Because of this, some problems will not be satisfactorily addressed by therapeutic modalities that rely exclusively on the hylotropic mode. The holotropic mode provides access to healing processes that complement those available to normal consciousness. Like many transpersonalists, Grof notes that these processes have been understood by the shamanic traditions, but have been overlooked or even despised by most of contemporary Western medicine and psychotherapy, and he believes that there is an urgent need for them to be integrated with it.

Ken Wilber: transpersonal levels

Ken Wilber (1979, 1981a) points out that most of the world's spiritual traditions recognize that there are several levels of the transpersonal domain. Drawing on Hindu concepts, he describes five of them. The 'low subtle' level mediates the kind of experiences we call para-normal, and that are often described by spiritual healers: telepathy, clairvoyance, out-of-body experiences and the ability to experience energy fields and channels within and around the body. The 'high subtle' mediates the kinds of experiences described by Jung: mythic imagery, archetypal experiences, spirit guides and deities. At the 'low causal' level experience changes radically: what was experienced as 'other' at the high subtle level is now experienced as part of oneself – instead of feeling awe before a deity, it is as if one becomes the deity. At the 'high causal' level, one's self is experienced as transcending all the forms of the subtle level, and all images fall away. Finally, there is the 'ultimate level', where all separation between subject and object is transcended, all levels are experienced as fundamentally the same and 'the entire world process is . . . experienced moment to moment as one's own being' (Wilber 1979: 8).

These levels are not like the steps of a ladder, but are nested hier-archically within one another. Wilber (1998) therefore refers to the 'Great Nest of Being', a term that is a modification of the more tra-ditional term 'Great Chain of Being' (see Chapter 2, p. 17). From the vantage point of the lower order nests, the higher order nests are completely hidden and unknown. However, as one learns to stabilize awareness within the higher order nests, the perceptions and sensitiv-ities of the lower level remain understandable and available. Wilber (1979, 1981a, 1981b, 1998) notes that different spiritual traditions propose different numbers of levels and give them different names. However, this is often because a tradition may specialize at one level and break it up into sub-levels, and not all traditions understand the higher levels. The phenomenology ascribed to a specific level within a specific tradition will usually allow it to be mapped on to the kind of scheme outlined above. This provides a framework for ordering the range of experiences described in Grof's cartography and in the texts of spiritual traditions. It also helps to resolve some paradoxes, because what seems true at one level does not seem true at another, and because the experiences of the higher levels seem fundamentally incompre-hensible when one's consciousness is at a lower level. For example, the high subtle experience of awe before a numinous presence (a divinity or saint) holds a central place in most religious traditions. However,

from the high subtle level, the causal level experience of dissolving into
the deity and becoming divine may sound shocking and be labelled
blasphemous. Many shamans and spiritual healers, for example, seem
to have integrated the low subtle level into their everyday experience
and are aware of consciously interacting with subtle energy fields.
Much of Jung's psychology and life experience revolved around the
high subtle level. Many spiritual teachings also seem to emanate from
this level. By looking at the content of spiritual teachings one can
identify the level of the hierarchy that is being explicated.

Huston Smith (1964: 93) discusses whether spiritual experiences
induced by psychedelic drugs are comparable to those reported
in the spiritual traditions. He argues that they are comparable as
experiences, but he observes that 'drugs appear able to induce
religious experiences; it is less evident that they can produce religious
lives'. 'Religious lives' seem to call for an integration of the insights
from these creative moments into one's everyday waking experience.
For many people, experiences from the higher levels erupt into
awareness through dreams, in special moments of creativity or
intuition or as a result of practices that induce non-ordinary states
of consciousness. When this happens, their implications may not be
grasped; they may seem so 'other' that they are simply ignored, or
they may be dismissed as hallucinations or dreams. Alternatively,
such experiences may act like a kind of call. Intrigued by the possibility they represent, individuals may change their lives in pursuit
of understanding and realization of their meaning and in due
course stabilize their everyday experience at a higher level. In Jung's
terms, this is the process of individuation, which calls not just
for an encounter with the unconscious, but for a sustained dialogue
with it (see Chapter 3, pp. 45–7). If they are to give rise to balanced
'religious lives', spiritual experiences (whether drug induced or from
any other source) need to be complemented by a spiritual tradition or
spiritual orientation to life that supports reflection and self-discipline.
Furthermore, those outstanding individuals who offer meaningful
spiritual leadership to their communities also show great intelligence
and imagination (Wulff 2000).

Michael Washburn: the spiral path of transpersonal development

Wilber's theory can be interpreted to mean that individuals will,
given the right conditions, progress smoothly from level to level

of the transpersonal hierarchy as if climbing a ladder. Such a steady progression can be observed in the lives of some individuals, such as the Indian saint Swami Muktananda, whose biography is examined by Mann (1984). For Muktananda, the right conditions involved spending several years in secluded meditation practice under the guidance of an experienced teacher. However, most people do not embark on the transpersonal phase of development at all, and those who do typically do not reach the ultimate level described by Wilber. Typically, the path of spiritual development 'is a long and arduous adventure, a journey through strange lands, full of wonders, but also beset with difficulties and dangers' (Assagioli 1991: 116).

To account for this, Washburn describes a three-phase developmental model that integrates concepts from Freud, Jung, object relations theory and Wilber (1979). At birth, although there are rudimentary ego structures, infants are immersed in a transpersonal matrix that he calls the 'dynamic ground' (Washburn 1988) or the 'non-egoic core' (Washburn 1994). This is not simply the product of biological instinctual processes, but is a dynamic source of 'neutral psychic energy . . . that empowers all psychic systems, processes and experiences, whether lower or higher, merely biological or spiritual' (Washburn 1988: 21). It therefore comprehends everything that Freud ascribed to the id and Jung to the collective unconscious. Wilber (1979) calls it the 'archaic unconscious'. At this stage, infants have a symbiotic relationship with mother and only experience limited aspects of this unconscious ground. Wilber calls this the experience of a body-self, which is similar to what Freud meant by 'libidinous'. In due course, as egoic structures develop, and children learn to function independently in the world, they must take the step of 'primal repression' (Washburn 1994: 24). This involves pulling out the plug from this energetic source, and breaking out of the state of 'original embedment' (Washburn 1988: 17). In the process, they sever their connectedness with mother and relate to others as a separate, circumscribed self. This creates a state of 'primal alienation' (Washburn 1994: 24), which becomes their mode of existence from then on.

Primal repression gives rise to 'the submerged unconscious' (Washburn 1988: 129); Wilber (1979) called it the 'submergent unconscious'. This is the defensively excluded material of the psychoanalysts' dynamic unconscious and of Jung's shadow. However, there is another route whereby material fails to reach awareness. A person's character is shaped by attitudes, assumptions and automatic habits of cognition and affect management. These in turn give rise to a moment-to-moment perceptual and cognitive filtering of information. Washburn (1988: 135), following Wilber (1979), refers to these aspects as the 'embedded unconscious'. This coincides with the prereflective unconscious of Stolorow and Atwood (see Chapter 5).

At this point in development there is a major difference between the psychoanalytic and transpersonal perspectives. Psychoanalysis focuses on stabilizing the second phase of development. This involves bringing to consciousness whatever has become problematic for ego-functioning, with the aim of neutralizing the affective charge of submerged material and softening the rigidity of embedded material. However, for transpersonal theorists, a third developmental phase is possible. The potential inherent in the transpersonal phase may present itself in various ways: through dreams, synchronistic experiences, intuitions or creative experiences, or through a chronic feeling of dissatisfaction with ordinary life. This is the call that comes from what Wilber (1979) refers to as the 'emergent unconscious', and Washburn (1994: 237) the 'deep unconscious'. This is not simply the return of repressed and unresolved infantile and childhood experiences. It is an invitation to a radical loosening of primal repression and a reopening of experience to the non-egoic core. It is an opportunity to move towards a resolution of the intrinsic tension created by the persistence of primal repression.

This involves a systematic dismantling of the separation from the non-egoic core that took place in childhood, and that has been the familiar mode of life for years and maybe for decades. Therefore, the process is far from a simple step up to another level. In reconnecting with the dynamic ground several kinds of problems typically arise. First, all the unresolved dilemmas of the phase of original embedment re-emerge and must be renegotiated. This calls for 'regression in the service of transcendence' (Washburn 1994: 26). Second, the energies of the core may be overwhelmingly intense and give rise to grandiose overestimation of one's abilities and worth (inflation), which in turn may result in loss of judgement in everyday situations. Third, as intense experiences pass, there may be disappointment and disillusionment because these experiences are mistaken for enlightenment, and are not recognized as being simply part of the process of reconnecting with the non-egoic core. Fourth, spontaneous visionary experiences such as those described in Grof's cartography may occur and be profoundly confusing to someone who does not have a road map and a guide.

Joseph Campbell (1956) showed how mythic tales of the hero's journey from many cultures express the turmoil and challenges of this transformative process. An individual leaves home on a quest (to find treasure, to rescue a prisoner), which represents the search for reconnection with the non-egoic core. To accomplish this, challenging tasks must be undertaken and huge obstacles overcome (impenetrable castle walls, monstrous foes, hazardous landscapes), which represent the forces previously excluded from awareness by primal repression. The exhaustive nature of the transformation process is often symbolized by an episode of dismemberment or death, which represents the complete dissolution of the egoic self. This is followed by restoration or resurrection, which represents rebirth into a new mode of being. The Sumerian Inanna has all her jewellery and clothes removed and is hung on a cross in the underworld. After three days she is rescued and restored (Eliade 1987a). The Egyptian Osiris is murdered and dismembered into 14 parts, which are collected and reassembled by his sister Isis (Eliade 1987b). The Greek bull god Dionysus Zagreus is dismembered and eaten by the Titans. Zeus keeps his heart, from which a new Dionysus is created (Gimbutas 1974). Myths of dismemberment are widespread in shamanic traditions across many cultures and commonly occur in the dreams and visionary experiences of contemporary individuals undergoing shamanic training (Harner 1995). Once the quest is achieved, the hero (or heroine) returns home, bringing gifts or jewels to the people. He (or she) lives as an ordinary person again, but contributes to society in new ways that bring healing or wisdom. This symbolizes the stage of spiritual integration: the individual's personal life can now be lived in fluid connection with the wider forces of the non-egoic core.

This transformational process can repeat itself as development proceeds through the transpersonal levels. Spiritual development is therefore often described as a 'spiral path of regression, regeneration and higher integration' (Washburn 1994: 239). After one stage of the spiral, individuals can mistakenly think that they have reached the goal. They may need a teacher to tell them that they are still on the journey and that the integration they have reached is no more than a stage. The possibilities of the deep unconscious are not finally realized until what Wilber calls the ultimate level is reached and integrated. Only here, where all distinctions between subject and object fall away, has separation from the source been finally dissolved. Consciousness has re-awakened 'to its absolutely prior and eternal abode as spirit, radiant and all-pervading' (Wilber 1981a: 41).

The emergent unconscious: science or faith?

A recurrent theme in transpersonal discourses is that we cannot normally conceive of the full range of possibilities for human growth and development. Our consciousness is profoundly limited, not only because of the kind of repressed and embedded material that other therapies focus upon, but because our everyday awareness can barely begin to comprehend the depth and nature of that hidden ground upon which our life is founded. Before the emergent mysteries that open up to the 'eye of contemplation' (see Chapter 7, p. 103), the habits of propositional knowing, which are the structures within which psychological theory is normally rendered, will inevitably falter. Bennet (1986: 17) puts these words into the mouth of Poshaiankia, the mythological father of Zuni shamanism:

> Our thoughts and the thoughts of our Grandfathers move like ripples on a pond throughout the Unknowable . . . Man [*sic*] must take his lead . . . from his unconscious, and have his actions and thoughts be true to it. That is the duty of us all, to live our outer lives in the service of our inner lives and thus in the service of the Unknowable.

Similarly, Hillman (1997: 285) points to the paradoxes inherent in a transpersonal approach:

> Humans ever and again try to crack the soul's code, to unlock the secrets of its nature. But what if its nature is not natural and not human? Suppose what we seek is not only something else, but somewhere else, in fact having no 'where' at all despite the call that beckons us to search. There is therefore nowhere to look beyond the fact of the call.

Transpersonal discourses make radical claims about the limitations of our everyday awareness, and about the kinds of awareness that are possible, if conditions are right. For those who do not find a transpersonal orientation compelling, these perspectives seem far-fetched, unscientific and more like a religious faith than a psychological theory. Those who are drawn to a transpersonal perspective, however, believe that there are significant human experiences that cannot be understood in any other way, and that approaches that settle for anything less will inevitably provide an incomplete account of human nature and the possibilities of human consciousness.

CHAPTER 8

Conscious and unconscious: the next hundred years

The study of the unconscious has the potential to become a unifying force in psychology, linking cognition and emotion,
infancy and old age, normal and pathological development,
brain and psyche.

(Bornstein and Masling 1998: xxi)

[The] evolved design of the emotion-processing mind suggests
that ... both survival and reproductive fitness were and are
served by nature's selecting for the reduction of conscious
knowledge of the enormously complex emotionally charged
environments faced by humans.

(Langs 1996: 96)

[The] history of science has involved a progressive extension of
the field concept to all the natural phenomena that used to be
explained in terms of souls.

(Sheldrake 1992: 86)

'Oh! It's about how some things are unconscious and others are subconscious,' remarked a guest at a dinner party whom one of us (DE)
was telling about this book. She expressed a common-sense view that
there are gradations in the ease with which we can bring different
aspects of psychological life to awareness. How simple it would be to
use 'subconscious' and 'unconscious' to label these gradations! DE
began to explain how James's and Janet's preference for the term *subconscious* was rooted in the ideological separation between mental
and brain processes, and that others, including Freud and Jung, had

referred to the same phenomena using the term 'unconscious' (see Chapter 2). He quickly realized that she was losing interest. She was perhaps thinking, 'You psychologists make everything unnecessarily complicated.' The conversation moved on to other things. Examination of how psychological understanding of conscious and unconscious is contained within a plurality of competing discourses, which are in some degree of disarray, does not make good dinner party conversation! This story reminds us that the technical discourses of psychotherapy also compete with other, less formal discourses – those of everyday conversation, of non-psychologists writing on psychological themes and even of some psychologists with allegiance to no particular ideological position. Even James, Adler and Jung used the terms 'subconscious' and 'unconscious' interchangeably at times (see Chapters 2 and 3).

Key terms are also used inconsistently by philosophers and scientists. Recently, Taylor, a neuroscientist, proposed that

> the mind has three levels, nonconscious, unconscious, and conscious, with the last two comprising knowledge, emotion and drive and, in addition, the conscious level supporting thought.
>
> (Taylor 1999: 15)

Here 'nonconscious' refers to brain activities that can never come to consciousness and 'unconscious' to those that 'have been repressed ... but still influence our actions'. By contrast, Kihlstrom's (1987: 1450) 'taxonomy of nonconscious mental structures' includes, in addition to what is conscious: (a) 'the unconscious proper', which can never come to awareness; (b) 'preconscious declarative knowledge', which 'reside[s] on the fringes of consciousness' and can become conscious under certain circumstances'; and (c) 'subconscious declarative knowledge', which is 'dissociated from phenomenal awareness' (Kihlstrom 1999: 436). For Kihlstrom, therefore, '*non*conscious' covers the entire domain, while Taylor's '*non*conscious' coincides with Kihlstrom's '*un*conscious proper'. Taylor's 'unconscious' conflates what for Freud were dynamically and descriptively unconscious, which means that he uses 'repressed' imprecisely. His use of the terms 'knowledge' and 'thought' also oversimplifies matters: first, because much of our implicit understanding of the world is inaccurate and so can hardly be called knowledge; second, because there is no clear boundary between thoughts that are conscious and other cognitions that are not. Kihlstrom does follow Freud in separating preconscious from warded off material, but because of his ideological preference for Janet's formulations and an apparent distaste for Freud, opts for the metaphor of dissociation rather than repression, and follows James and Janet in using 'subconscious' rather than 'unconscious'. These inconsistencies and differences are presented here to show how today, just as was the case a century ago, in this highly significant area of psychology discourse politics still abound and no common language has been adopted by the scientific community.

Conscious, unconscious and language

Further conceptual problems arise because the term 'conscious' has several different meanings. First, it means 'present to phenomenal awareness'. This is the meaning that lies behind Freud's distinction between conscious and preconscious, or applies when a person with blindsight is described as able to discriminate between two visual patterns without being conscious of them (Chapter 6, p. 93). This definition is too simple to cope with demonstrations of implicit learning, where research participants are conscious of the light flashes, but have no awareness of the nature of the learning process, or of what they have learned. The debate over whether implicit learning is really 'unconscious' (Chapter 6, p. 96) betrays a confusion about the meaning of the term 'conscious'. This not only indicates that something registers in phenomenal awareness, but also refers to its being rendered into a comprehensible verbal account. Freud was partly aware of the role of language in making something conscious. In his 1915 paper on 'The unconscious', he wrote:

> What . . . repression denies to the rejected presentation . . . [is] translation into words which shall remain attached to the object. A presentation which is not put into words . . . remains thereafter in the *Ucs* in a state of repression.
>
> (Freud 1915b: 202)

However, Freud's understanding is less clear than ours today, because it is founded on his distinction between primary and secondary process, in which he equates 'conscious' with secondary process, which in turn is equated with language. In terms of the concepts presented in Chapter 5, Freud confuses the dynamic unconscious (created by active warding off) and the prereflective unconscious (not yet formulated in language), a criticism levelled at him by Adler.

The fact that 'unconscious' can mean unformulated in language also explains Freud's (1923a: 21) paradoxical remark that 'thinking in pictures is . . . a very incomplete form of becoming conscious [which] stands nearer to unconscious processes than does thinking in words'. He was pointing, of course, to the 'primary process' character of imagery. Today we might instead say that though visual images are present to phenomenal awareness, their underlying meanings are often not verbally formulated.

Implicit learning is unconscious in two ways: individuals cannot give a verbal account of how the learning took place or of what they actually learned. They can learn to make what they learned 'conscious' in that they can learn to state the rules explicitly. However, they cannot become conscious of the learning process itself. Like researchers in linguistics who formulate (and thus make conscious) the underlying principles of language that most people follow automatically, psychotherapists help their clients to develop a coherent verbal account of the implicitly learned patterns that govern their interpersonal relationships and ways of dealing with everyday situations. But these insights say little about the actual process of implicit learning, a point to which we now turn.

Conscious but hollow: the paradox of insight

Insights that are formulated in words during psychotherapy can sometimes be life-changing, while at other times they have no impact. Suppose a woman, who has had a series of unsatisfactory relationships with gentle, passive and indecisive men, arrives at the insight: 'I can see how I have been attracted to men who are quite different from my father, as if I have been working to avoid dealing with the ways he hurt me, but somehow I end up getting hurt anyway.' Or perhaps the insight is first formulated like this by the therapist. If she becomes tearful and feels relief, this is because an unconsciously enacted pattern has at last 'become conscious', and she can begin to free herself from its self-defeating grip. However, what if she responds with a blank look or feels irritated or misunderstood? This could mean the therapist was wrong. But it could also be that the client is not yet ready to assimilate the insight: from a psychoanalytic perspective, she is resistant; from a cognitive perspective she cannot yet tolerate the cognitive dissonance that would be evoked. In this case, the insight has not become conscious for the client even though the therapist has put it into words. As Adler put it, it is still 'not understood'.

Even where it is apparently understood, will the insight lead to significant change in the client's future behaviour? Sometimes clients seem to grasp an insight intellectually but it 'has a hollow feel' (Kriegman 1998: 241) and the critical change processes fail to occur. The insight may even consolidate the existing behaviour patterns as the client tells her friends about how she cannot deal with relationships with strong men because of how she was treated by her father. In this case, she can hardly be said to have made the unconscious conscious, since she has only assimilated the insight superficially into the consciously held narrative of her life, and has left untouched the implicit learning that is at the root of her problems. Something more is needed. Psychoanalytic therapists might invite her to focus on facing those past hurts, 'working them through' in the therapeutic relationship and learning to find a new and more positive relational experience; cognitive therapists might encourage her to 'emotionally reprocess' them and recommend she experiment with new ways of behaving in significant relationships. These therapeutic endeavours, which work directly at the implicit level without necessarily consciously formulating everything in words, can lead to a re-organization of the deep relational schemas that Bollas (1987: 36) calls 'the grammar of our being' (see Chapter 5, p. 79).

Mindfulness: a different kind of awareness

This suggests that there are a variety of ways of being 'conscious' of something. The point is often made by teachers of a form of Buddhist meditation designed to develop 'mindfulness'. The practice involves sitting quietly, paying attention gently and easily to physical sensations, emotions, thoughts or images as they arise from moment to moment, and noting them without judgement or attachment. Mindfulness does not involve intellectual formulation or conscious reflection. It is the cultivation of a mode of 'being' rather than 'doing' (Segal *et al.* 2002). This promotes something whose value Adler and cognitive behaviour therapists have emphasized: interrupting the automaticity that characterizes everyday modes of living. As a mode of awareness it is the opposite to 'mindlessness', a state in which one is caught up unreflectively in the stream of mental and behavioural activity. Meditators learn how to observe psychological states neutrally and avoid identifying with them, in the same way one might watch a cloud passing across the sky. Mindfulness also involves letting go of the defensiveness that characterizes everyday experience:

unpleasant and unsettling material is quietly observed, rather than pushed away, or the process of pushing it away can itself come under observation. This can be challenging, since it requires a willingness to experience painful emotions.

Martin (1997) suggests that most forms of psychotherapy involve a cultivation of this kind of experiencing, although the term 'mindfulness' is not necessarily used. In psychoanalysis, both therapist and client are encouraged to cultivate such non-defensive awareness: this characterizes free association, and the 'state of evenly suspended attention' that Freud (1923b: 239) recommended for therapists. Similarly, cognitive therapists encourage their clients to 'decentre' from automatic patterns of thought and feeling, and avoid 'personalizing' them or identifying with them. A growing literature explores the value and significance of mindfulness for psychotherapy, not only in transpersonal psychology (Walsh 1977, 1978; Kornfield 1986), but also in psychoanalysis (Epstein 1983, 1986; Engler 1984) and cognitive therapy (Marlatt and Kristeller 1999; Segal *et al.* 2002).

Mindfulness meditation helps practitioners to become 'more conscious' in several senses. First, they notice experiences that previously they would not have given any attention to; second, it helps them to allow repressed material to emerge into awareness; third, as a consequence of gaining insight into how conditioned, automatic, irrational and driven is their normal functioning, they can 'wake up' as if out of a trance, and find a new mode of experiencing that is at the same time more detached but also more present to the moment. Meditators also report spontaneous and meaningful insights that permanently alter their perspectives on life, evidence that the practice can instigate a reorganization of tacit knowledge structures in the absence of any deliberate intention to do so (Walsh 1977, 1978; Tart 1986).

'The . . . unconscious' as a discourse tool

Phrases of the form 'the . . . unconscious', which first became popular in nineteenth-century Germany (see Chapter 2), serve as a tool for discourse in a variety of ways. Terms like 'the collective unconscious', 'the dynamic unconscious', 'the heterosexist unconscious' or the 'emergent unconscious' do not usually indicate that a precise map is being offered of a specific 'domain' or 'part of the mind'. They function instead as discourse markers indicating that what are being addressed are unconscious influences on experience and/or behaviour which share some broad commonality. The ' . . . ' in these phrases points in the direction of the nature of that commonality. These phrases also imply that what is being referred to affects everyone in a similar way. Thus a term like 'the heterosexist unconscious' suggests that we are all influenced by a hidden matrix of the same kind of gendered assumptions. This is why Reid (1999: 58), who warns of the effect of 'unconscious cultural values' on the perspectives and feelings of clients, does not speak of a 'cultural unconscious'. His emphasis is on the diversity of the 'hidden cultures' (1999: 64) within which clients and therapists are inevitably embedded. Apparent 'resistance' from clients and failures of empathy by therapists often stem from the 'culture blindness' (1999: 78) unwittingly instilled by psychotherapy training, which fails to alert trainees to the subtle impacts of the multiplicity of cultural perspectives.

These phrases, together with others such as 'the unconscious mind' or 'the subconscious mind', exercise a strong fascination, since they imply something powerful, mysterious and beyond our control. This is why, in hypnotherapy, suggestions may be given that the client is allowing his or her unconscious mind to assume control (see Example 8 in Chapter 1, p. 10). Discourses with an advocacy agenda draw on this fascination when they use phrases like 'the heterosexist unconscious'. The message is, 'Here are hidden forces that deeply affect us and that we ignore at our peril.' Roszak (1993, 1994) uses 'the ecological unconscious' and Aizenstat (1995: 95) the 'world unconscious' in this way, warning of the dangers posed by threats to the environment. This is also a transpersonal concept, an aspect of the collective unconscious that 'shelters the compacted ecological intelligence of our species' (Roszak 1993: 306). Like the ancient concept of *anima mundi* (world soul: see Chapter 7, pp. 105–6), it refers to an underlying holistic field within which 'all creatures and things of the world are interrelated and connected' (Aizenstat 1995: 95–6). Through attuning to this field, individuals can experience the world not, as they normally do, in terms of the values of human material comfort and the single-minded promotion of economic growth, but in terms of the needs of all species on the planet. This presents a new perspective on the struggles and suffering of other life forms resulting from human activities that are systematically damaging the ecosystems on which they depend, and causing an accelerating extinction of species.

The ecological unconscious is generally part of the shadow (in Jung's terms). We keep it unconscious because it is painful to recognize our alienation from nature and the harm our species is perpetrating. However, this alienation creates its own pain. 'The voice of the earth is that close by,' writes Roszak (1993: 305), 'if we are, as the Romantic poets believed, born with the gift of hearing that voice, then turning a deaf ear to her appeal . . . must be painful.' Ecopsychologists point to several ways of creating dialogue with the ecological unconscious. Wilderness retreats provide a means of fostering empathic attunement to the natural world. When we 'step into the looking glass of nature and contact wilderness,' writes Harper (1995: 185), 'we uncover a wisdom much larger than our small everyday selves'. They also promote confrontation with the unacknowledged pain either on the retreat itself or when individuals return to the everyday world and see afresh the ecological insensitivity that characterizes the way we mostly live (Greenway 1995). Dreams (Aizenstat 1995) and psychotherapy methods that induce altered states of consciousness (Grof 1998) can also give rise to encounters with the ecological unconscious, and integration of these experiences can significantly enhance individual awareness and concern regarding ecological issues.

Bynum (1999) uses the concept of 'the African unconscious' to advocate an imaginative foundation for the dignity of black people and to shake up Western stereotypes of 'Black' and 'African'. Drawing on palaeontological and genetic research, which has provided major advances in the understanding of the evolution of our species, he concludes that all of us 'are interwoven on the loom of a primordial African unconscious' (Bynum 1999: xxv). This is because our species evolved in Africa: four million years ago, the *australopithecines* began walking upright; two and a half million years ago, *Homo habilis*, with a markedly larger brain, made use of tools; some 1.7 million years ago, the more advanced *Homo erectus* could use fire and was the first hominid species to venture outside Africa. Our own species, *Homo sapiens*, evolved in East Africa some 300,000 years ago; perhaps only 90,000 years ago, a small number made it out of Africa, where they consolidated a genetic heritage that would serve as the basis for the species in the rest of the world. There is evidence of *Homo sapiens* in Malaysia 75,000 years ago, and in Australia shortly after that. By 30,000 years ago they had spread to South America, Western Europe, Northern Russia and Japan (Caird 1994). The separation of races, with their distinctive hair, skin colour and facial and bodily features, has been under way for less than 100,000 years and perhaps as little as 30,000. 'Before that', Bynum (1999: 11) suggests, 'all humankind was dark-skinned and Africoid.'

Bynum's 'African unconscious' also connotes the personal

and spiritual qualities that mark a distinctively African mode of experience. From this perspective, all things are experienced as interconnected and energized by an underlying life force; an affinity for rhythm, both bodily and musically, finds spontaneous expression in healing rituals; and consciousness is communally oriented rather than individualistic. Paradoxically, it can be thought of both as *unconscious*, in that it is experienced without being reflected on, and as a distinctive mode of shared *consciousness*. While this may be the lived experience of black (African) people, for Europeans it is part of the shadow, in Jung's sense. For centuries, Europeans have culturally repressed dimensions of psychological experience associated with their African roots and despised Africans and other blacks as primitive, emotionally uninhibited and lacking in intelligence. For Westerners to reconnect with their repressed African unconscious, argues Bynum, would offer a much needed correction to the materialistic and driven modes of consciousness that dominate their culture.

Bynum's African unconscious also has transpersonal aspects. The values and perspectives associated with it are, he believes, transmitted not only genetically and culturally, but also through an interactive field that functions 'like a conscious and living world Internet' (Bynum 1999: 100). Furthermore, he sees it as the basis for the potential for human spiritual transformation. The ancient Egyptians believed that a spiritual world underlies the world of appearances, and that individuals can become profoundly transformed if they engage in the right kinds of spiritual practice. These ideas, argues Bynum, were essentially an African discovery that developed within the first human civilization, which began to establish itself in Nubia and Egypt in the Nile Valley, some 15,000 years ago.

Bynum's arguments could throw light on a famous dream of Jung's. He was deeply affected by the silence and spaciousness of Africa, as well as by the natural dignity of the Africans themselves. During his 1925 visit, he dreamed of an American Negro barber who was making his hair black and curly. The image frightened Jung and he interpreted it as a warning that he must not allow himself to be swept away from his European roots: 'the primitive was a danger to me. At that time I was obviously all too close to "going back"' (Jung 1977: 302). Jung's life was lived in dialogue with the deep spiritual heritage that Bynum subsumes under 'the African unconscious'; and we have seen the affinities between his approach to psychotherapy and the practices of shamans (see Chapter 7). That he could so strongly recoil from whatever it was that he experienced as 'primitive' might indeed indicate an alienation from some ancient roots that is deeply embedded in European civilization.

Many of Bynum's concerns and perspectives coincide with those of other writers. Metzner (1994), for example, has pointed out how shamanic practices have been suppressed in the West for some 2000 years and points to the history of persecution of so-called 'witches' and practitioners of natural healing. He shares with Bynum the view that contemporary interest in ancient spiritual practices can be understood as a 'return of the repressed' at a collective level. While Bynum uses these ideas to promote a consciousness (or an unconscious) that is specifically black or African, Metzner (1993) offers them as a focus for revisioning the nature of 'European consciousness'. Bynum's interweaving of so many diverse themes under the rubric of 'the African unconscious' can best be understood as the imaginative forging of a contemporary myth of origin for Africans and those of African descent, a myth that could serve to enhance the dignity, integrity and spiritual purpose of contemporary black people. It reveals the flexibility of the formula 'the . . . unconscious' as a tool of human discourse and the complexity that can lie hidden below the surface of a simple phrase. With such a Protean face, it seems likely that the form 'the . . . unconscious' will still be widely used a century from now.

A hundred years of scientific research

Bornstein and Masling's view, cited at the head of this chapter, that the study of the unconscious could become a unifying force, rather than (as it has often been) a divisive one, is based on the impact of advances across a range of scientific disciplines. Cognitive scientists present increasingly subtle demonstrations of unconscious influences on awareness and behaviour (see Chapter 6), and sophisticated developmental research on attachment patterns in infants and young children is increasingly integrated into theories of psychotherapy (see Chapter 5). Compared to a century ago, we have a far more differentiated knowledge of the brain and of how its pathways and structures work together to manage perception and control behaviour. Studies such as those with individuals with 'blindsight' (see Chapter 6, p. 93) do not support the view that consciousness is simply an emergent property of brains once they reach a certain level of complexity. They suggest that conscious awareness depends on quite specific parts of the brain, and that it can be decoupled from the capacity to make sensory discriminations. Neuroimaging techniques using PET scanning show which parts of the brain are activated when different tasks are performed or different experiences reported. Such studies 'may be on the brink of revealing [brain] structures which may have a unique role to play in the conscious awareness of sensory events' (Weiskrantz 1997: 214).

We also have a more comprehensive understanding of the evolution of our species (aspects of the latter stages of which were summarized above). We know that much of our everyday information processing is based on structures and mechanisms that we share with other living creatures, and is not part of the special systems that mediate reflective consciousness. This perspective is contributing to the theoretical convergence between what were, in the past, differing ideological points of view. It increasingly informs the cognitive-behavioural literature and served as the focus of a special issue of the *Journal of cognitive psychotherapy* edited by Gilbert (2002). The concept of the 'cognitive unconscious' was first introduced to refer to mechanisms that are very ancient and do not necessarily depend on a cerebral cortex, such as those that enable bees to communicate about the location of nectar. An evolutionary perspective has also contributed to the understanding of anxiety, which is managed by mechanisms that evolved in environments very different from those most people inhabit today. Since they are highly automated, there are significant limitations on our capacity to bring them under strategic control. Although there may be a role for reflective discussion in treatment, lasting change often depends on interventions involving behavioural exposure (see Chapter 6, p. 97, and Hoffman, Moscovitch and Heinrichs 2002).

Psychoanalytic formulations are also being re-examined from an evolutionary perspective. Kriegman (1998) points out the implications of natural selection for attributions about motivation. Behaviours that have been selected through evolution have a cause that is *distal* (the evolutionary advantage), but this does not necessarily imply a *proximal* cause in the form of a specific intention, either conscious or unconscious. For example, women's behaviour in making themselves attractive to men makes sense from an evolutionary point of view, since women who attracted powerful men had a reproductive advantage. Thus, when a woman dresses in such a way that males find her sexually attractive (the evolutionary argument supposes that this male response has also been naturally selected), this does not imply a proximal motivation, conscious or even unconscious, to elicit sexual arousal in men. She is automatically doing what women have been genetically programmed to do. From this perspective, we could perhaps reinterpret Schopenhauer's phrase 'the unconscious will in nature' (see Chapter 2, p. 21) to mean that the goal directedness is 'in nature' (i.e. in natural selection) rather than necessarily in the motivation of specific individuals. When an attractively dressed woman is told by a man that she is obviously wanting sex, or by a male therapist that she is consciously or unconsciously trying to seduce him, she will rightly experience the situation as abusive. This kind of interpretation, Kriegman observes, has been an unfortunate part of the history of psychoanalysis and is based on the erroneous view that 'stimulating raw, male lust, to the degree that men actually are stimulated to experience it, is the unconscious wish in women'. More likely, he concludes, this interpretation is simply 'a projection of men's desire' (Kriegman 1998: 215).

A feature of hominid evolution has been the increased immaturity and vulnerability of new born infants, and the long period before children reach adulthood. To ensure survival, human groups needed to be cohesive over long periods. This end was served by the strengthening and deepening of parent–child attachment bonds and by children becoming adapted to accommodating the dictates of their caretakers. This is best achieved, suggests Kriegman, 'by allowing only the acceptable parts of one's potential personality to be seen by others. The rest is best kept out of awareness where one's own self-knowledge cannot betray its existence' (1998: 226–7). Group cohesiveness is also served in so far as this accommodation to the group continues into adulthood. Thus repression and self-deception have obvious evolutionary advantages. It would not, however, be adaptive for repressed parts of the self to simply be erased. Circumstances can change dramatically. Motivations, emotions and behaviours that are repressed to accommodate one setting could be life-saving in other contexts, where they might 'provide for an expanded repertoire of adaptive behaviors and more flexible (adaptive) ways of organizing experience' (1998: 231). This puts an unexpected perspective on repression. If natural selection is the distal cause of repression and self-deception, the presence of these behaviours does not imply a proximal motivation, conscious or unconscious, to repress or deceive intentionally. It is natural (because naturally selected) for these behaviours to occur automatically without intention or insight. The processes that underlie repression are unconscious because they are automatic and do not involve consciously mediated strategic processes. This offers a powerful refutation of the criticism Sartre and Boss levelled at Freud, that the self-deception involved in repression must at some level be intentional and conscious (see Chapter 4, p. 50).

Langs provides another reason why repression is adaptive. As increased intelligence and the development of language enhanced the capacity for emotional differentiation and sensitivity, *Homo sapiens* was routinely faced with a complex array of difficult 'emotionally charged impingements' (Langs 1996: 134). Furthermore, with the development of intelligence and foresight, and the deepening of attachments, the anticipation of one's own death and that of one's loved ones became unbearably painful. In addition, 'a deep unconscious fear-guilt subsystem' (1996: 170) evolved to provide a protective mechanism against the risk of individuals becoming violent and murderous towards their own family and group members. For all of this activity of 'the emotion processing mind' to remain conscious would overload the conscious system, which was essential for ensuring individual and group survival. Consequently, the 'conscious defensiveness' (1996: 154), which is so often a central focus of psychotherapy, became an evolutionary necessity. Natural selection favoured minds that were split and that perceived and processed emotionally salient meanings outside of awareness. This is why psychotherapy is so challenging, Langs suggests; its goal is to overcome the defensiveness that evolution has painstakingly built into human nature!

However, some provision was made for the expression of the split-off contents of the emotion-processing mind. Language-based thought developed two distinctive modes: a 'paradigmatic/scientific mode 'served science and our search for logical truths and led to the emergence of a *theoretic culture*', while a narrative mode, through which 'shared anxieties and adaptive issues were dealt with by collective story-telling and myths of origin, death, warfare, kinship, and much more', provided the basis for a *'mythic culture'* (1996: 132, original italics). These narratives indirectly express, and provide a vehicle for processing, the emotional conflicts and dilemmas that are not addressed directly in everyday conversation. Langs points out the serious disadvantages of this arrangement and concludes that 'the design of the emotion-processing mind is ... fundamentally flawed' (1996: 109). Unconscious emotions give rise to projection and distorted perceptions, so that 'an enormous number of behaviours ... are unwittingly dislocated from their true origins and therefore misapplied and maladaptive. We are remarkably unaware of the deep motives related to much of our emotional lives' (1996: 170).

Thus, as a result of an evolutionary compromise, which secured advantages to the species only at great cost, it is the human existential predicament to suffer from 'the inherited disease of a dysfunctional emotion-processing mind' (1996: 194). As Gilbert (2002: 266) observes, 'Evolved design is not, necessarily good design.'

Of all contemporary formulations, Langs's perspective seems particularly close to the spirit of Freud. Freud recognized how myth and drama revealed the nature of the unconscious. 'Here are my masters', he said in 1926, as he showed a visitor the works of Shakespeare and the Greek tragedians on his shelves (Ellenberger 1970). Langs criticizes contemporary psychoanalysts: 'the fundamentals of the emotion-processing mind have gone virtually unrecognized . . . Indeed the entire realm of deep unconscious experience has been neglected' (Langs 1996: 200). This, of course, is the criticism Freud levelled at Adler a little less than a century ago (see Chapter 3, pp. 38–9).

Implicational meaning: narrative, poetry and myth

Like Langs, Teasdale (1996) argues that there are two parallel and distinct cognitive modes of encoding meaning into language (see Chapter 1, p. 5). He calls these propositional (Langs's theoretic) and implicational (Langs's mythic). Because the systems are functionally separate, changes in one system do not necessarily generalize to the other. This means that evolution also lies behind the familiar dilemma that we examined above: that apparently helpful insights in psychotherapy turn out to be hollow in terms of promoting meaningful change. Making something conscious in the sense that it is rendered in propositional code may not address meaning at the implicit or implicational level.

Teasdale also points out that, by their very nature, propositional formulations never fully capture the subtleties and nuances that can be conveyed by implicational expression. This is why poetry can often convey something that cannot be easily explained in propositional code. This is explored in the film *Il Postino*. Mario befriends the poet Pablo Neruda and gradually becomes intrigued by his encounter with poetry. On one occasion, Mario tells Neruda how a line in his poem has expressed an aspect of his experience that he could not himself have put into words: 'I liked it too when you wrote, "I'm tired of being a man." That's happened to me too, but I never knew how to say it. I really liked it when I read it.'

Then he asks Neruda to explain another line, 'the smell of barber shops makes me sob out loud'. But Neruda refuses. 'I can't tell you in words different from those I've used. When you explain it, poetry becomes banal.' Psychotherapy techniques that use expressive methods involving poetry, dramatization, imagery and metaphor (Edwards 1990; Lyddon and Alford 2000; Bolton 2001) work directly with mythic or implicational language. These not only capture the richness of implicational meaning, but can also contribute to changing it, without having to explain it. Langs's use of clients' narratives of everyday events as communications that automatically encode deep unconscious meanings (see Chapter 5) is another way of working directly at the implicational level.

A poem by South African poet Don Maclennan (2002) similarly highlights some of these aspects of implicational language:

Poems are nets of thought
put out to catch
what can be sensed only
in a corner of the mind.
A poem never drains
its ground of silence.
Poems make you
see and touch and smell:
they bring the world closer
so you can live in it again.

Unformulated experiences can be disturbing in two ways: first, we are separated from them because we have not integrated them; second, they demand our attention because, in Perls's language, they press to emerge out of the background and become figure. Allowing them into the foreground and finding words for them undoes our sense of separation and 'bring[s] the world closer'. However, whether in poetry or psychotherapy, even the implicational use of words cannot ever tell the full story; there will always be an irreducible 'silence' that eludes their grasp.

Evolution, natural selection and the transpersonal unconscious

Finally, we turn to one of the most persistent theoretical conflicts to which the science of evolution has given rise, and one that bears directly on significant aspects of the psychology of the unconscious.

Natural selection selects for genes, and genes do not alter during an individual's lifetime. Therefore, individuals may genetically pass on aptitudes or personality traits, but not life experience or memories. Without the complex mechanisms of cultural transmission, specific skills, ways of thinking or images would not pass on to another generation. While a great deal of work remains to be done, most unconscious psychological processes we have examined in this book seem to be approachable within an evolutionary framework based on natural selection. However, the kinds of phenomena that led Jung to posit a collective unconscious involve the transmission of images in a way that cannot be explained by genetic transmission.

The vivid imagery associated with psychotic hallucinations or drug-induced altered states of consciousness often contains detailed mythological material from cultures completely unfamiliar to the individual concerned. Thus, Jung (1952) describes a patient in a Swiss hospital who saw the sun with a phallus, which was the source of the wind. Only later did Jung discover this was an image from the liturgy of the Roman god Mithras. Grof's description of a psychedelic experient's vision of the Malelukan pig goddess (see Example 10 in Chapter 1, p. 13) provides another example of this phenomenon. While apparent regressions into past lives can often easily be shown to be constructions based on cryptamnesia (Spanos *et al.* 1991), this is by no means always the case. In 1987, one hypnotherapy client experienced an apparent 'past life' as a submariner who died with his ship in 1942; he provided detailed names and dates that could be confirmed from the records of the naval base where he was supposed to have served (Brown 1991). If we insist on a Darwinian account, these phenomena must be examples of cryptamnesia, suggestion or fraud. These individuals *must* have encountered the images or information before even if they had forgotten where. Because of the diverse range of cultural material most people are exposed to, it is usually difficult to exclude these explanations. However, Jung, who understood the nature of cryptamnesia (see Chapter 3, p. 42), is only one of many who have believed they have encountered cases where cryptamnesia is an implausible explanation.

The biological concept of morphic fields offers a theory that is consistent with natural selection and provides for the transmission of memories and images in a way that could explain these kinds of anomalous data. According to the hypothesis of formative causation, several biological phenomena, including aspects of learning and human behaviour, can only be fully explained if we suppose that the biochemical processes set in motion by the genes interact with morphic fields (Sheldrake 1985, 1992). For example, in the development of a human body from conception to adulthood, genetic theory explains how the raw materials for human form are inherited, but the detailed process by which they give rise to a differentiated human body depends on morphogenetic fields, which are a kind of morphic field. To use an analogy, in building a house, the genes explain how the raw materials get to the building site, and the field explains how they get to be assembled into a properly functioning house.

Sheldrake (1989) hypothesizes that morphic fields are also involved in the formation of behavioural and cognitive patterns, both across evolutionary time and within the life of the individual. They could allow us to explain how blind termites can work together to construct a coherent system of burrows in a mound and how flocks of birds and shoals of fish can move together in coherent unison. These fields evolve and grow with the evolution of a species:

> They contain a kind of collective memory on which each member of the species draws and to which it in turn contributes . . . The fields are the means by which the habits of the species are built up, maintained and inherited.
>
> (Sheldrake 1992: 109–10)

As individuals learn new habits, these are transmitted to the morphic field, which has the effect of enabling other members of the species to acquire the habits faster. If this is the case, we can understand the brain not in terms of the metaphor of a computer that contains all the information and algorithms necessary to manage behaviour and acquire new learning, but at least in part as a TV receiver that tunes into morphic fields, and by a process of morphic resonance, receives information from and gives information to them.

These hypotheses are controversial, of course. An anonymous reviewer in *Nature* referred to one of Sheldrake's books as an 'infuriating tract . . . [that is] . . . the best candidate for book burning there has been for many years' (Sheldrake 1985: dustwrapper). If leading figures within science make rules about what may be written or spoken about, then, to use Billig's (1999) terms, its conversations will create their own unconscious, the shadow cast over anomalous phenomena that are not supposed to be there. Transpersonal theorists (Singer 1990; Bolen 1993; Grof 1998) find Sheldrake's ideas attractive because they address the kind of paradoxical data that they encounter in their work and for which they do not believe that cryptamnesia or suggestion provide adequate explanations. Whatever the language in which they speak of it, transpersonal theories conceive of the unconscious as an active domain with a life of its own, which is ultimately mysterious and unknowable. The concept of morphic fields is complex enough to support this perspective since each species has its own field, as does each member of the species, and within this complex hierarchical arrangement, the fields interact with each other. Since they evolve over time, they provide a basis for Jung's recognition of the significance of history for understanding the unconscious (see Chapter 3, pp. 41 and 44).

Might this theory have appealed to Freud? Although he is not usually thought of as a transpersonal theorist, there are transpersonal aspects to some of his less popularized views (see Chapter 3, pp. 47–8). His concept, which has been translated into English as 'id', is taken from Georg Groddeck's (1923) *The Book of the It* (German *Es*), which we cited at the start of Chapter 1. Groddeck presents the 'It' as a mysterious matrix with a life of its own; and many of the things he attributes to it have strong affinities to Sheldrake's theory. Freud (1933: 55) also wondered about 'how the common purpose comes about in the great insect communities', and wondered if this was based on 'a direct psychical transference'. Sheldrake argues that morphic fields can account for these kinds of phenomena. Finally, Freud, who paid much attention to clients' imagery, also concluded that, although it did not fit with Darwinian theory, there must be transmission of ancestral memory traces. 'I cannot do without this factor in biological evolution', he remarked uncompromisingly (Freud 1939: 100).

Conclusion

We have now seen what a wide range of phenomena is addressed by the idea of an unconscious or of unconscious psychological processes. These include activities orchestrated by automatic processes that never reach consciousness at all; basic learning processes involving implicit mechanisms that do not involve conscious intention; material kept out of awareness by the automatic processes of repression and self-deception, or by dissociative processes resulting from trauma; the hidden effects of social factors such as culture, gender and power relations; and experiences that point to a deeper underlying transpersonal matrix. The kinds of field theory proposed by Bohm and Pribram (see Chapter 7, p. 107) and by Sheldrake point towards the possibility of developing a unified scientific framework that could accommodate all the different aspects of unconscious psychological life we have encountered in this book, and that would be both scientifically testable and psychologically meaningful. Will that be the achievement of the next century? Or will the authors of a book like this, a hundred years from now, still be reporting on a plurality of discourses and on the competition and conflicts between them, in much the same way as we have done here in our exploration of how psychotherapists of the past hundred years have conceptualized and debated the dialectical relationship between conscious and unconscious in psychotherapy.

References

Adler, A. (1911) The psychic treatment of trigeminal neuralgia, in *The Practice and Theory of Individual Psychology* (trans. P. Radin, 1929). London: Kegan Paul, Trench, Trubner and Co.

Adler, A. (1912a) Psychical hermaphrodism and the masculine protest – the cardinal problem of nervous diseases, in *The Practice and Theory of Individual Psychology* (trans. P. Radin, 1929). London: Kegan Paul, Trench, Trubner and Co.

Adler, A. (1912b) *The Neurotic Constitution* (trans. B. Glueck and J. Lind, 1921). London: Kegan Paul, Trench, Trubner and Co.

Adler, A. (1913a) Individual-psychological treatment of neuroses, in *The Practice and Theory of Individual Psychology* (trans. P. Radin, 1929). London: Kegan Paul, Trench, Trubner and Co.

Adler, A. (1913b) On the role of the unconscious in neurosis, in *The Practice and Theory of Individual Psychology* (trans. P. Radin, 1929). London: Kegan Paul, Trench, Trubner and Co.

Adler, A. (1930) *The Science of Living*. London: George Allen and Unwin.

Adler, A. (1932) *What Life Should Mean to You* (ed. A. Porter). London: George Allen and Unwin.

Adler, A. (1938) *Social Interest: A Challenge to Mankind* (trans. J. Linton and R. Vaughan). London: Faber and Faber.

Aizenstat, S. (1995) Jungian psychology and the world unconscious, In T. Roszak, M. E. Gomes and A. D. Kanner (eds) *Ecopsychology: Restoring the Earth, Healing the Mind*. San Francisco: Sierra Club Books.

Alford, B. A. and Beck, A. T. (1997) *The Integrative Power of Cognitive Therapy*. New York: Guilford.

American Psychiatric Association (2000) *DSM-IV-TR: Diagnostic and Statistical Manual of Mental Disorders*, 4th edn: Text revision Washington, DC: American Psychiatric Association.

Andrews, B., Brewin, C. R., Ochera, J., Morton, J., Bekerian, D. A., Davies,

G. M. and Mollon, P. (2000) The timing, triggers and qualities of recovered memories in therapy, *British Journal of Clinical Psychology*, 39: 11–26.

Ansbacher, H. L. and Ansbacher, R. R. (1958) *The Individual Psychology of Alfred Adler: A Systematic Presentation in Selections from His Writings*. London: George Allen and Unwin.

Assagioli, R. (1965) *Psychosynthesis*. London: Turnstone.

Assagioli, R. (1991) *Transpersonal Development: The Dimension beyond Psychosynthesis*. London: Crucible.

Baars, B. J. (1997) In the theatre of consciousness: global workspace theory, a rigorous scientific theory of consciousness, *Journal of Consciousness Studies*, 4: 292–309.

Bandura, A. (1986) *Social Foundations of Thought and Action: A Social Cognitive Theory*. Englewood Cliffs, NJ: Prentice Hall.

Bandura, A. (1997) *Self-efficacy: The Exercise of Control*. New York: W. H. Freeman.

Bargh, J. A. and Chartrand, T. L. (1999) The unbearable automaticity of being, *American Psychologist*, 54: 462–79.

Bartlett, F. C. (1932) *Remembering*. London: Cambridge University Press.

Beck, A. T. and Clark, D. M. (1997) An information processing model of anxiety: automatic and strategic processes, *Behaviour Research and Therapy*, 35: 49–58.

Beck, A. T. and Emery, G. (1985) *Anxiety Disorders and Phobias: A Cognitive Approach*. New York: Basic Books.

Beck, A. T., Rush, A. J., Shaw, B. F. and Emery, G. (1979) *Cognitive Therapy of Depression*. New York: John Wiley.

Beck, J. S. (1995) *Cognitive Therapy: Basics and Beyond*. New York: Guilford.

Bem, D. J. and Honorton, C. (1994) Does psi exist? Replicable evidence for an anomolous process of information transfer, *Psychological Bulletin*, 115: 4–18.

Bennet, H. Z. (1986) *Inner Guides, Visions, Dreams and Dr Einstein*. Berkeley, CA: Celestial Arts.

Berne, E. (1975) *What Do You Say after You Say Hello?* London: Corgi.

Billig, M. (1999) *Freudian Repression: Conversation Creating the Unconscious*. Cambridge: Cambridge University Press.

Bohm, D. and Hiley, B. J. (1983) *The Undivided Universe: An Ontological Interpretation of Quantum Theory*. London: Routledge.

Bolen, J. S. (1993) Synchronicity and the tao: mysticism, metaphor, morphic fields and the quest for meaning, *ReVision*, 16: 8–14.

Bollas, C. (1987) *The Shadow of the Object: Psychoanalysis of the Unthought Known*. New York: Columbia University Press.

Bolton, G. (2001) The blood jet is poetry (Plath, 1981), *Clinical Psychology*, 7: 39–42.

Boorstein, S. (1995) *Transpersonal Psychotherapy*, 2nd edn. Palo Alto, CA: Science and Behavior Books.

Bornstein, R. F. and Masling, J. M. (1998) *Empirical Perspectives on the Psychoanalytic Unconscious*. Washington, DC: American Psychological Association.

Boss, M. (1963) *Psychoanalysis and Daseinsanalysis*. New York: Dacapo Press (new edition 1982).

Boss, M. (1977) *I Dreamt Last Night*. New York: Gardner Press.

Boss, M. (1986) The unconscious – what is it?, *Review of Existential Psychology and Psychiatry*, 20: 237–49.

Bowers, K. S. and Meichenbaum, D. (eds) (1984) *The Unconscious Reconsidered*. New York: John Wiley.

Bowlby, J. (1979) *The Making and Breaking of Affectional Bonds*. London: Tavistock.

Bowra, C. M. (1961) *The Romantic Imagination*. London: Oxford University Press.

Brennan, B. A. (1998) *Hands of Light*. New York: Bantam.

Breuer, J. (1895) Studies on hysteria. III, Theoretical, in *The Standard Edition of the Complete Psychological Works of Sigmund Freud, Volume 2*. London: Virago (2001 edn).

Brewin, C. (1988) *Cognitive Foundations of Clinical Psychology*. Hove: Lawrence Erlbaum Associates.

Brewin, C. R. and Andrews, B. (1998) Recovered memories of trauma: phenomenology and cognitive mechanisms, *Clinical Psychology Review*, 18: 949–70.

Broughton, R. (1986) Human consciousness and sleep/waking rhythms, in B. B. Wohlman and M. Ullman (eds) *Handbook of States of Consciousness*. New York: Van Nostrand Reinhold.

Brown, R. (1991) The reincarnation of James – the submarine man, *Journal of Regression Therapy*, 5: 62–71.

Browne, I. (1990) Psychological trauma, or unexperienced experience, *ReVision*, 12: 21–34.

Bührmann, M. V. (1984) *Living in Two Worlds: Communication between a White Healer and Her Black Counterparts*. Wilmette, IL: Chiron.

Burns, D. D. (1990) *The Feeling Good Handbook*. New York: Plume.

Burston, D. (1986) The cognitive and dynamic unconscious – a critical and historical perspective, *Contemporary Psychoanalysis*, 22: 132–56.

Bynum, E. B. (1999) *The African Unconscious*. New York: Teacher's College Press.

Caird, R. (1994) *Ape Man: The Story of Human Evolution*. London: Boxtree.

Campbell, J. (1956) *The Hero with a Thousand Faces*. New York: Meridian.

Cardeña, E., Lynn, S. J. and Krippner, S. (2000) *The Varieties of Anomolous Experience*. Washington, DC: American Psychological Association.

Chadwick, H. (1991) *Saint Augustine Confessions*. Oxford: Oxford University Press.

Chalmers, D. J. (1996) *The Conscious Mind*. New York: Oxford University Press.

Child, I. L. (1985) Psychology and anomolous observations: the question of ESP in dreams, *American Psychologist*, 40: 1219–30.

Clark, D. M. (1997) Panic disorder and social phobia, in D. M. Clark and C. G. Fairburn (eds) *The Science and Practice of Cognitive Behaviour Therapy*. Oxford: Oxford University Press.

Clark, D. M. and Fairburn, C. G. (eds) (1997) *The Science and Practice of Cognitive Behaviour Therapy*. Oxford: Oxford University Press.

Cloitre, M. (1992) Avoidance of emotional processing, in D. Stein and J. E. Young (eds) *Cognitive Science and Clinical Disorders*. San Diego: Academic Press.

Cohen, M. B. (1953) Introduction, in H. S. Sullivan, *The Interpersonal Theory of Psychiatry*. New York: W. W. Norton.

Colby, K. M. (1958) Discussion of Adler's ideas by Freud and others, in H. L. Ansbacher and R. R. Ansbacher (eds) *The Individual Psychology of Alfred Adler: A Systematic Presentation in Selections from His Writings*. London: George Allen and Unwin.

Coleman, D. G. (1987) *Montaigne's Essais*. London: Allen and Unwin.

Conkling, M. (1986) Sartre's refutation of the Freudian unconscious, *Review of Existential Psychology and Psychiatry*, 20: 251–65.

Craighead, W. E., Kazdin, A. E. and Mahoney, M. J. (1976) *Behavior Modification: Principles, Issues and Applications*. Boston: Houghton Mifflin.

Cushman, P. (1990) Why the self is empty: toward a historically situated psychology, *American Psychologist*, 45: 599–611.

Davies, J. M. (1998) Multiple perspectives on multiplicity, *Psychoanalytic Dialogues*, 8: 195–206.

Davies, J. M. and Frawley, M. G. (1999) Dissociative processes and transference–countertransference paradigms in the psychoanalytically oriented treatment of adult survivors of sexual abuse, in S. A. Mitchell and L. Aron (eds) *Relational Psychoanalysis: The Emergence of a Tradition*. Hillsdale, NJ: Analytic Press.

Doore, G. (ed.) (1988) *Shaman's Path: Healing, Personal Growth and Empowerment*. Boston: Shambala.

Dostoyevsky, F. (1868) *The Idiot*, trans. C. Garnett. London: William Heinemann (1913).

Dostoyevsky, F. (1876) *A Raw Youth*, trans. C. Garnett. London: William Heinemann Ltd (1916).

Dowd, E. T. (1992) Hypnotherapy, in A. Freeman and F. Dattilio (eds) *Comprehensive Casebook of Cognitive Therapy*. New York: Plenum.

Dowd, E. T. (2000) *Cognitive Hypnotherapy*. Northvale, NJ: Jason Aronson.

Dowd, E. T. and Courchaine, K. E. (1996) Implicit learning, tacit knowledge, and implications for stasis and change in cognitive psychotherapy, *Journal of Cognitive Psychotherapy*, 10: 163–80.

Eden, J. (1993) *Energetic Healing: The Merging of Ancient and Modern Medical Practices*. New York: Plenum.

Edwards, D. J. A. (1990) Cognitive therapy and the restructuring of early memories through guided imagery, *Journal of Cognitive Psychotherapy*, 4: 33–51.

Eliade, M. (ed.) (1987a) *Encyclopedia of Religion, Volume 11*. New York: Macmillan.

Eliade, M. (ed.) (1987b) *Encyclopedia of Religion, Volume 7*. New York: Macmillan.

Ellenberger, H. F. (1970) *The Discovery of the Unconscious: The History and Evolution of Dynamic Psychiatry.* New York: Basic Books.

Ellis, A. (1973) *Humanistic Psychotherapy.* New York: McGraw-Hill.

Ellis, A. (1989) Rational-emotive therapy, in R. J. Corsini and D. Wedding (eds) *Current Psychotherapies,* 4th edn. Itasca IL: F. E. Peacock.

Engler, J. (1984) Therapeutic aims in psychotherapy and meditation: developmental stages in the representation of the self, *Journal of Transpersonal Psychology,* 16: 25–62.

Epstein, M. (1983) The deconstruction of the self: ego and 'egolessness' in Buddhist insight meditation, *Journal of Transpersonal Psychology,* 20: 61–9.

Epstein, M. (1986) Meditative transformations of narcissism, *Journal of Transpersonal Psychology,* 18: 143–59.

Epstein, S. (1998) Cognitive-experiential self theory: a dual process personality theory with implications for diagnosis and psychotherapy, in R. F. Bornstein and J. M. Masling (eds) *Empirical Perspectives on the Psychoanalytic Unconscious.* Washington, DC: American Psychological Association.

Fancher, R. E. (1979) *Pioneers of Psychology.* New York: W. W. Norton.

Faraday, A. (1975) *The Dream Game.* London: Maurice Temple Smith.

Ferenczi, S. (1915) Psychogenic anomalies of voice production, in J. Rickman (ed.) *Further Contributions to the Theory and Technique of Psycho-analysis.* New York: Brunner/Mazel (trans. J. I. Suttie and others, 1926, reprinted 1980).

Ferenczi, S. (1929) The principle of relaxation and neocatharsis, in M. Balint (ed.) *Final Contributions to the Problems and Methods of Psycho-analysis.* New York: Brunner/Mazel (trans. E. Mosbacher and others, 1955, reprinted 1980).

Ferenczi, S. (1931) Child analysis in the analysis of adults, in M. Balint (ed.) *Final Contributions to the Problems and Methods of Psycho-analysis.* New York: Brunner/Mazel (trans. E. Mosbacher and others, 1955, reprinted 1980).

Ferenczi, S. (1933) Confusion of tongues between adults and the child, in M. Balint (ed.) *Final Contributions to the Problems and Methods of Psychoanalysis.* New York: Brunner/Mazel (trans. E. Mosbacher and others, 1955, reprinted 1980).

Foa, E. B. and Kozak, M. J. (1986) Emotional processing of fear: exposure to corrective information, *Psychological Bulletin,* 99: 20–35.

Fourcher, L. A. (1992) Interpreting the relative and absolute unconscious, *Psychoanalytic Dialogues,* 2: 317–29.

Frame, D. M. (1955) *Montaigne's Discovery of Man.* New York: Columbia University Press.

Frankel, F. H. (1994) Dissociation in hysteria and hypnosis: a concept aggrandized, in S. J. Lynn and J. W. Rhue (eds) *Dissociation: Clinical and Theoretical Perspectives.* New York: Guilford.

Frankl, G. (1994) *Exploring the Unconscious: New Pathways in Depth Analysis.* London: Open Gate Press.

Freud, S. (1893) A case of successful treatment by hypnotism, in *The Standard Edition of the Complete Psychological Works of Sigmund Freud, Volume 1.* London: Virago (2001 edn).

Freud, S. (1894) The neuropsychoses of defence, in *The Standard Edition of the Complete Psychological Works of Sigmund Freud, Volume 3*. London: Virago (2001 edn).

Freud, S. (1895a) Studies on hysteria: case histories (3) Miss Lucy R, in *The Standard Edition of the Complete Psychological Works of Sigmund Freud, Volume 2*. London: Virago (2001 edn).

Freud, S. (1895b) Studies on hysteria: Case histories (5) Fraulein Elizabeth von R, in *The Standard Edition of the Complete Psychological Works of Sigmund Freud, Volume 2*. London: Virago (2001 edn).

Freud, S. (1895c) Studies on hysteria. IV, The psychotherapy of hysteria, in *The Standard Edition of the Complete Psychological Works of Sigmund Freud, Volume 2*. London: Virago (2001 edn).

Freud, S. (1896) Further remarks on the neuro-psychoses of defence, in *The Standard Edition of the Complete Psychological Works of Sigmund Freud, Volume 3*. London: Virago (2001 edn).

Freud, S. (1900a) *The Standard Edition of the Complete Psychological Works of Sigmund Freud, Volumes 4 and 5: The Interpretation of Dreams*. London: Virago (2001 edn).

Freud, S. (1901) *The Standard Edition of the Complete Psychological Works of Sigmund Freud, Volume 6: The Psychopathology of Everyday Life*. London: Virago (2001 edn).

Freud, S. (1905) *The Standard Edition of the Complete Psychological Works of Sigmund Freud, Volume 8: Jokes and Their Relation to the Unconscious*. London: Virago (2001 edn).

Freud, S. (1910) Five lectures on psychoanalysis, in *The Standard Edition of the Complete Psychological Works of Sigmund Freud, Volume 11*. London: Virago (2001 edn).

Freud, S. (1911) Great is Diana of the Ephesians, in *The Standard Edition of the Complete Psychological Works of Sigmund Freud, Volume 12*. London: Virago (2001 edn).

Freud, S. (1912) A note on the unconscious in psychoanalysis, in *The Standard Edition of the Complete Psychological Works of Sigmund Freud, Volume 12*. London: Virago (2001 edn).

Freud, S. (1914) On the history of the psychoanalytic movement, in *The Standard Edition of the Complete Psychological Works of Sigmund Freud, Volume 14*. London: Virago (2001 edn).

Freud, S. (1915a) Repression, in *The Standard Edition of the Complete Psychological Works of Sigmund Freud, Volume 14*. London: Virago (2001 edn).

Freud, S. (1915b) The unconscious, in *The Standard Edition of the Complete Psychological Works of Sigmund Freud, Volume 14*. London: Virago (2001 edn).

Freud, S. (1920) Beyond the pleasure principle, in *The Standard Edition of the Complete Psychological Works of Sigmund Freud, Volume 18*. London: Virago (2001 edn).

Freud, S. (1923a) The ego and the id, in *The Standard Edition of the Complete Psychological Works of Sigmund Freud, Volume 19*. London: Virago (2001 edn).

Freud, S. (1923b) Two encyclopedia articles: (A) psychoanalysis, in *The Standard Edition of the Complete Psychological Works of Sigmund Freud, Volume 18*. London: Virago (2001 edn).

Freud, S. (1926) Inhibitions, symptoms and anxiety, in *The Standard Edition of the Complete Psychological Works of Sigmund Freud, Volume 20*. London: Virago (2001 edn).

Freud, S. (1927) Fetishism, in *The Standard Edition of the Complete Psychological Works of Sigmund Freud, Volume 21*. London: Virago (2001 edn).

Freud, S. (1930) Letter to Dr Alfons Paquet, in *The Standard Edition of the Complete Psychological Works of Sigmund Freud, Volume 21*. London: Virago (2001 edn).

Freud, S. (1933) New introductory lectures on psychoanalysis. Lecture XXX: Dreams and occultism, in *The Standard Edition of the Complete Psychological Works of Sigmund Freud, Volume 22*. London: Virago (2001 edn).

Freud, S. (1939) Moses and monotheism: Three essays, in *The Standard Edition of the Complete Psychological Works of Sigmund Freud, Volume 23*. London: Virago (2001 edn).

Freud, S. (1940) Splitting of the ego in the process of defence, in *The Standard Edition of the Complete Psychological Works of Sigmund Freud, Volume 23*. London: Virago (2001 edn).

Gay, P. (1989) *Freud: A Life for Our Time*. London: Papermac.

Gendlin, E. T. (1978) *Focusing*. New York: Everest House.

Gendlin, E. T. (1996) *Focusing-oriented Psychotherapy: A Manual of the Experiential Method*. New York: Guilford.

Gilbert, P. (2002) Evolutionary approaches to psychopathology and cognitive therapy. *Journal of Cognitive Psychotherapy*, 16(3): 263–94.

Gimbutas, M. (1974) *The Gods and Goddesses of Old Europe 7000–3500 BC: Myths, Legends and Cult Images*. London: Thames and Hudson.

Goldberg, A. (1999) *Being of Two Minds: The Vertical Split in Psychoanalysis and Psychotherapy*. New York: Tarcher/Putnam.

Goldfried, M. R. (1995) *From Cognitive-behavior Therapy to Psychotherapy Integration: An Evolving View*. New York: Springer.

Grant, J. and Crawley, J. (2002) *Transference and Projection*. Buckingham: Open University Press.

Gray, J. A. (1995) Consciousness – what is the problem and how should it be addressed?, *Journal of Consciousness Studies*, 2: 5–9.

Greenberg, L. S. and Safran, J. D. (1984) Integrating affect and cognition: a perspective on the process of therapeutic change, *Cognitive Therapy and Research*, 8: 559–78.

Greenberg, R. L. (1997) Depression, in R. Leahy (ed.) *Practicing Cognitive Therapy: A Guide to Interventions*. Northvale, NJ: Jason Aronson.

Greenwald, A. (1992) New look 3: unconscious cognition reclaimed, *American Psychologist*, 47: 766–77.

Greenway, R. (1995) The wilderness effect and ecopsychology, in T. Roszak, M. E. Gomes and A. D. Kanner (eds) *Ecopsychology: Restoring the Earth, Healing the Mind*. San Francisco: Sierra Club Books.

Groddeck, G. W. (1923) *The Book of the IT*. London: Vision Press (trans. 1949, reprinted 1979).

Grof, S. (1976) *Realms of the Human Unconscious*. Pomona: Hunter House.

Grof, S. (1985) *Beyond the Brain: Birth, Death and Transcendence in Psychotherapy*. Albany, NY: SUNY Press.

Grof, S. (1998) *The Cosmic Game: Explorations of the Frontiers of Human Consciousness*. Albany, NY: SUNY Press.

Grotstein, J. S. and Rinsley, D. B. (1994) *Fairbairn and the Origins of Object Relations*. London: Free Association Books.

Guidano, V. F. and Liotti, G. (1983) *Cognitive Processes and Emotional Disorders*. New York: Guilford.

Hackmann, A. (1997) The transformation of meaning in cognitive therapy, in M. J. Power and C. Brewin (eds) *The Transformation of Meaning in Psychological Therapies: Integrating Theory and Practice*. Chichester: John Wiley.

Harner, M. (1990) *The Way of the Shaman*, 3rd edn. San Francisco: Harper and Row.

Harner, M. (1995) The myth of shamanic dismemberment. Paper presented at the Fourteenth Conference of the International Transpersonal Association, Santa Clara, CA.

Harper, S. (1995) The way of wilderness, in T. Roszak, M. E. Gomes and A. D. Kanner (eds) *Ecopsychology: Restoring the Earth, Healing the Mind*. San Francisco: Sierra Club Books.

Harris, A. (1998) Aggression: pleasures and dangers. *Psychoanalytic Inquiry*, 18: 31–44.

Hillman, J. (1991) *A Blue Fire: Selected Writings by James Hillman Introduced and Edited by Thomas Moore*. New York: HarperPerennial.

Hillman, J. (1997) *The Soul's Code: In Search of Character and Calling*. London: Bantam.

Hirsch, I. and Roth, J. (1995) Changing conceptions of the unconscious, *Contemporary Psychoanalysis*, 31: 263–76.

Hoffman, S. G., Moscovitch, D. A. and Heinrichs, N. (2002) Evolutionary mechanisms of fear and anxiety. *Journal of Cognitive Psychotherapy*, 16(3): 317–30.

Holmes, C. (1999) Confessions of a communicative psychotherapist, in E. M. Sullivan (ed.) *Unconscious Communication in Practice*. Buckingham: Open University Press.

Horner, A. J. (1987) The unconscious and the archaeology of human relationships, in R. Stern (ed.) *Theories of the Unconscious and Theories of the Self*. Hillsdale, NJ: Analytic Press.

Huxley, A. (1946) *The Perennial Philosophy*. London: Chatto and Windus.

Issacharoff, A. and Hunt, W. (1994) Transference and projective identification, *Contemporary Psychoanalysis*, 30: 593–604.

Ivey, G. (2001) Projective identification – do we really need it? Paper presented at the First South African Conference for Psychotherapy organized by the South African Association for Psychotherapy, Rhodes University, Grahamstown.

Jacoby, L. L., Lindsay, S. D. and Toth, J. P. (1992) Unconscious influences revealed: awareness, attention and control, *American Psychologist*, 47: 802–9.

James, W. (1891) *Principles of Psychology, Volume 1*. London: Macmillan.

James, W. (1902) *The Varieties of Religious Experience*. New York: Longmans, Green, and Co.

James, W. (1993) The varieties of consciousness: observations on nitrous oxide, in R. Walsh and F. Vaughan (eds) *Paths beyond Ego: The Transpersonal Vision*. Los Angeles: Jeremy P. Tarcher/Perigee (first published 1902).

Janet, P. (1924) *Principles of Psychotherapy* (trans. H. M. and E. R. Guthrie). London: George Allen and Unwin.

Jung, C. G. (1902) On the psychology and pathology of so-called occult phenomena, in *The Collected Works of C. G. Jung, Volume 1: Psychiatric Studies*, 2nd edn. London: Routledge and Kegan Paul.

Jung, C. G. (1905) The reaction time ratio in the association experiment, in *The Collected Works of C. G. Jung, Volume 2: Experimental Researches*, 2nd edn. London: Routledge and Kegan Paul.

Jung, C. G. (1906) The psychopathological signficance of the association experiment, in *The Collected Works of C. G. Jung, Volume 2: Experimental Researches*, 2nd edn. London: Routledge and Kegan Paul.

Jung, C. G. (1930) Problems of modern psychotherapy, in *The Collected Works of C. G. Jung, Volume 16: The Practice of Psychotherapy: Essays on the Psychology of the Transference and Other Subjects*, 2nd edn. London: Routledge and Kegan Paul.

Jung, C. G. (1931a) Basic postulates of analytical psychology, in *The Collected Works of C. G. Jung, Volume 8: The Structure and Dynamics of the Psyche*, 2nd edn. London: Routledge and Kegan Paul.

Jung, C. G. (1931b) The structure of the psyche, in *The Collected Works of C. G. Jung, Volume 8: The Structure and Dynamics of the Psyche*, 2nd edn. London: Routledge and Kegan Paul.

Jung, C. G. (1934) The relations between the ego and the unconscious, in *The Collected Works of C. G. Jung, Volume 7: Two Essays on Analytical Psychology*, 2nd edn. London: Routledge and Kegan Paul.

Jung, C. G. (1935) Principles of practical psychotherapy, in *The Collected Works of C. G. Jung, Volume 16: The Practice of Psychotherapy: Essays on the Psychology of the Transference and Other Subjects*, 2nd edn. London: Routledge and Kegan Paul.

Jung, C. G. (1939) Conscious, unconscious and individuation, in *The Collected Works of C. G. Jung, Volume 9, Part 1: The Archetypes of the Collective Unconscious*, 2nd edn. London: Routledge and Kegan Paul.

Jung, C. G. (1942) The psychology of the unconscious, in *The Collected Works of C. G. Jung, Volume 7: Two Essays on Analytical Psychology*, 2nd edn. London: Routledge and Kegan Paul.

Jung, C. G. (1946) Psychology of the transference, in *The Collected Works of C. G. Jung, Volume 16: The Practice of Psychotherapy: Essays on the Psychology of the Transference and Other Subjects*, 2nd edn. London: Routledge and Kegan Paul.

Jung, C. G. (1948) A review of the complex theory, in *The Collected Works of C. G. Jung, Volume 8: The Structure and Dynamics of the Psyche*, 2nd edn. London: Routledge and Kegan Paul.

Jung, C. G. (1950) *The Collected Works of C. G. Jung, Volume 9, Part 2: Aion: Researches into the Phenomenology of the Self*, 2nd edn. London: Routledge and Kegan Paul.

Jung, C. G. (1952) *The Collected Works of C. G. Jung, Volume 5: Symbols of Transformation: An Analysis of the Prelude to a Case of Schizophrenia*, 2nd edn. London: Routledge and Kegan Paul.

Jung, C. G. (1958a) Synchronicity: an acausal connecting principle, in *The Collected Works of C. G. Jung, Volume 8: The Structure and Dynamics of the Psyche*, 2nd edn. London: Routledge and Kegan Paul.

Jung, C. G. (1958b) The transcendent function, in *The Collected Works of C. G. Jung, Volume 8: The Structure and Dynamics of the Psyche*, 2nd edn. London: Routledge and Kegan Paul.

Jung, C. G. (1977) *Memories, Dreams, Reflections*. Glasgow: Collins Fount Paperbacks.

Kalweit, H. (1988) *Dreamtime and Inner Space: The World of the Shaman*. Boston: Shambhala.

Karagulla, S. (1967) *Breakthrough to Creativity: Your Higher Sense Perception*. Marina del Rey, CA: De Vorss.

Keller, E. F. (1985) *Reflections on Gender and Science*. New Haven, CT: Yale University Press.

Kernberg, O. F. (1976) *Object-relations Theory and Clinical Psychoanalysis*. New York: Jason Aronson.

Kernberg, O. F. (1987) The dynamic unconscious and the self, in R. Stern (ed.) *Theories of the Unconscious and Theories of the Self*. Hillsdale, NJ: Analytic Press.

Kihlstrom, J. F. (1984) Conscious, subconscious, unconscious: a cognitive perspective, in K. S. Bowers and D. Meichenbaum (eds) *The Unconscious Reconsidered*. New York: John Wiley.

Kihlstrom, J. F. (1987) The cognitive unconscious, *Science*, 237: 1445–52.

Kihlstrom, J. F. (1999) The psychological unconscious, in L. A. Pervin and O. P. John (eds) *Handbook of Personality: Theory and Research*, 2nd edn. New York: Guilford.

Kihlstrom, J. F., Mulvaney, S., Tobias, B. A. and Tobis, I. P. (2000) The emotional unconscious, in E. Eich, J. F. Kihlstrom, G. H. Bower, J. P. Forgas and P. M. Niedenthal (eds) *Cognition and Emotion*. Oxford: Oxford University Press.

Klein, D. B. (1977) *The Unconscious: Invention or Discovery? A Historico-critical Enquiry*. Santa Monica, CA: Goodyear.

Kohut, H. (1977) *The Restoration of the Self*. New York: International Universities Press.

Kornfield, J. (1986) Intensive insight meditation: a phenomenological study, *Journal of Transpersonal Psychology*, 11: 41–58.

Kriegman, D. (1998) Interpetation, the unconscious and analytic authority: toward an evolutionary biological integration of the empirical-scientific

method with the field-defining, empathic stance, in R. F. Bornstein and
J. M. Masling (eds) *Empirical Perspectives on the Psychoanalytic Unconscious*.
Washington, DC: American Psychological Association.

Kunz, D. and Peper, E. (1984a) Fields and their clinical implications. Part IV:
Depression from the energetic perspective – etiological underpinnings,
American Theosophist, 72: 268–75.

Kunz, D. and Peper, E. (1984b) Fields and their clinical implications. Part V:
Depression from the energetic perspective – treatment strategies, *American
Theosophist*, 72: 299–306.

Laing, R. D. (1965) Transcendental experience in relation to religion and
psychosis, in S. Grof and C. Grof (eds) *Spiritual Emergency: When Personal
Transformation Becomes a Crisis*. Los Angeles: Jeremy P. Tarcher.

Lane, R. D. and Schwartz, G. E. (1987). Levels of emotional awareness: a
cognitive-developmental theory and its application to psychopathology,
American Journal of Psychiatry, 144: 133–43.

Lane, R. D. and Schwartz, G. E. (1992) Levels of emotional awareness: Implications for psychotherapy integration, *Journal of Psychotherapy Integration*, 2:
1–18.

Langs, R. (1983) *Unconscious Communication in Everyday Life*. New York: Jason
Aronson.

Langs, R. (1996) *The Evolution of the Emotion-processing Mind*. London: Karnac
Books.

Layden, M. A., Newman, C. F., Freeman, A. and Morse, S. B. (1993) *Cognitive
Therapy of Borderline Personality Disorder*. Boston: Allyn and Bacon.

Layton, L. (1998) *Who's that Girl? Who's that Boy? Clinical Practice Meets
Postmodern Gender Theory*. Northvale, NJ: Jason Aronson.

Layton, L. (1999) Cultural hierarchies, splitting and the dynamic unconscious,
Paper presented at the 107th Annual Convention of the American
Psychological Association, Boston.

Leahy, R. (1996) *Cognitive Therapy: Basic Principles and Applications*. Northvale,
NJ: Jason Aronson.

Lewicki, P., Hill, T. and Czyzewska, M. (1992) Nonconscious acquisition of
information, *American Psychologist*, 47: 796–801.

Lombardi, K. (1998) Resurrecting the unconscious in contemporary psychoanalysis, in N. Rucker and K. Lombardi (eds) *Subject Relations: Unconscious
Experience and Relational Psychoanalysis*. New York: Routledge.

Lombardi, K. and Rucker, N. (1998) Sounds of silence: parallel dreaming and
the mutual dream, in N. Rucker and K. Lombardi (eds) *Subject Relations:
Unconscious Experience and Relational Psychoanalysis*. New York: Routledge.

London, P. (1972) The end of ideology in behavior modification, *American
Psychologist*, 27: 913–19.

Lyddon, W. J. and Alford, D. J. (2000) Metaphor and change in cognitive and
constructive psychotherapies. Paper presented at the World Congress of
Cognitive Therapy, Catania, Sicily.

McGinn, L. K. and Young, J. E. (1996) Schema-focused therapy, in P. Salkovskis
(ed.) *Frontiers of Cognitive Therapy*. New York: Guilford.

McGinn, L. K., Young, J. E. and Sanderson, W. C. (1995) When and how to do longer term therapy . . . without feeling guilty, *Cognitive and Behavioral Practice*, 2: 187–212.

McIntosh, D. (1995) *Self, Person, World: The Interplay of Conscious and Unconscious in Human Life.* Evanston, IL.: Northwestern University Press.

Mack, J. E. (1993) Foreword, in R. Walsh and F. Vaughan (eds) *Paths beyond Ego: The Transpersonal Vision.* Los Angeles: Jeremy P. Tarcher/Perigee.

Maclennan, D. (2002) *The Road to Kromdraai.* Cape Town: Snailpress.

McNally, R. J. (1995) Automaticity and the anxiety disorders, *Behaviour Research and Therapy*, 33: 747–54.

McNiff, S. (1992) *Art as Medicine.* Boston: Shambhala.

Mahler, M. D. (1979) *The Selected Papers of Margaret S. Mahler, MD, Volume II: Separation-individuation.* New York: Jason Aronson.

Mahoney, M. J. and Thoresen, C. E. (1974) *Self-control: Power to the Person.* Monterey: Brooks/Cole.

Mann, R. (1984) *The Light of Consciousness.* Albany, NY: SUNY Press.

Marlatt, G. A. and Kristeller, J. L. (1999) Mindfulness and meditation, in W. R. Miller (ed.) *Integrating Spirituality into Treatment: Resources for Practitioners.* Washington, DC: American Psychological Association.

Martin, J. R. (1997) Mindfulness: a proposed common factor, *Journal of Psychotherapy Integration*, 7: 291–312.

Masson, J. M. (1985) *The Assault on Truth.* Harmondsworth: Penguin.

Masters, J. C., Burish, T. G., Hollon, S. D. and Rimm, D. C. (1987) *Behavior Therapy: Techniques and Empirical Findings*, 3rd edn. San Diego: Harcourt, Brace, Jovanovich.

Masters, R. E. L. and Houston, J. (1966) *The Varieties of Psychedelic Experience.* London: Blond.

Meichenbaum, D. (1977) *Cognitive-behavior Modification: An Integrative Approach.* New York: Plenum.

Merleau-Ponty, M. (1942) *The Structure of Behavior* (trans. A. L. Fisher, 1967). Boston: Beacon.

Metzner, R. (1989) States of consciousness and transpersonal psychology, in R. S. Valle and S. Halling (eds) *Existential-phenomenological Perspectives in Psychology: Exploring the Breadth of Human Experience.* New York: Plenum.

Metzner, R. (1993) The split between spirit and nature in European consciousness, *ReVision*, 15: 177–85.

Metzner, R. (1994) *The Well of Remembrance: Rediscovering the Earth Wisdom Myths of Northern Europe.* Boston: Shambhala.

Miller, A. (1984) *Thou Shalt not Be Aware: Society's Betrayal of the Child.* New York: Farrar, Straus & Giroux.

Mintz, E. (1983) *The Psychic Thread: Paranormal and Transpersonal Aspects of Psychotherapy.* New York: Human Sciences Press.

Mitchell, S. A. and Aron, L. (1999) *Relational Psychoanalysis: The Emergence of a Tradition.* Hillsdale, NJ: Analytic Press.

Moore, T. (1992) *Care of the Soul: A Guide for Cultivating Depth and Sacredness in Everyday Life.* New York: HarperCollins.

Mullahy, P. (1970) *Psychoanalysis and Interpersonal Psychiatry: The Contributions of Harry Stack Sullivan*. New York: Science House.

Mutwa, V. C. (1996) *Song of the Stars: The Lore of a Zulu Shaman*. Barrytown, NY: Barrytown Ltd, Station Hill Openings.

Öhman, A. and Mineka, S. (2001) Fears, phobias and preparedness: Toward an evolved module of fear and fear learning. *Psychological Review*, 108: 483–522.

Padesky, C. A. (1996) *Guided Discovery: Using Socratic Dialogue* (Video). Newport Beach, CA: Center for Cognitive Therapy.

Perls, F. S. (1947) *Ego, Hunger and Aggression*. New York: Vintage Books (new edition 1969).

Perls, F. S. (1972) Four lectures, in J. Fagan and I. L. Shepherd (eds) *Gestalt Therapy Now*. Harmondsworth: Penguin.

Perls, F. S. (1973) *The Gestalt Approach and Eye-witness to Therapy*. New York: Bantam Books.

Polanyi, M. (1958) *Personal Knowledge: Towards a Post Critical Philosophy*. Chicago: University of Chicago Press.

Power, M. J. (1997) Conscious and unconscious representations of meaning, in M. J. Power and C. Brewin (eds) *The Transformation of Meaning in Psychological Therapies: Integrating Theory and Practice*. Chichester: John Wiley.

Pribram, K. (1986) The cognitive revolution and mind–brain issues, *American Psychologist*, 41: 507–19.

Putnam, F. W. (1989) *Diagnosis and Treatment of Multiple Personality Disorder*. New York: Guilford.

Reber, A. S. (1993) *Implicit Learning and Tacit Knowledge: An Essay on the Cognitive Unconscious*. Oxford: Oxford University Press.

Reid, T. (1999) A cultural perspective on resistance, *Journal of Psychotherapy Integration*, 9: 57–81.

Rennie, D. L. (2000) Aspects of the client's conscious control of the therapeutic process, *Journal of Psychotherapy Integration*, 10: 151–67.

Rice, S. (1981) *The Buddha Speaks Here and Now*. Kandy, Sri Lanka: Buddhist Publication Society.

Rogers, C. R. (1951) *Client-centered Therapy: Its Current Practice, Implications and Theory*. Boston: Houghton Mifflin.

Rogers, C. R. (1967) *On Becoming a Person: A Therapist's View of Psychotherapy*. London: Constable.

Rogers, C. R. (1973) Some new challenges, *American Psychologist*, 28: 379–87.

Rogers, N. (1999) The creative connection: a holistic expressive arts process, in S. K. Levine and E. G. Levine (eds) *Foundations of Expressive Arts Therapy*. London: Jessica Kingsley.

Romanyshyn, R. D. (1982) *Psychological Life: From Science to Metaphor*. Austin: University of Texas Press.

Ronen, T. (1997) *Cognitive Developmental Therapy with Children*. New York: Wiley.

Roszak, T. (1993) *The Voice of the Earth: An Exploration of Ecopsychology*. London: Bantam.

Roszak, T. (1994) Ecopsychology and the anima mundi, *ReVision*, 16: 108–15.

Rowan, J. (1993) *The Transpersonal: Psychotherapy and Counselling*. London: Routledge.

Rowan, J. and Jacobs, M. (2002) *The Therapist's Use of Self*. Buckingham: Open University Press.

Rozin, P. (1976) The evolution of intelligence and access to the cognitive unconscious, in E. Stellar and J. M. Sprague (eds) *Progress in Psychobiology and Physiological Psychology: Volume 6*. San Diego: Academic.

Rucker, N. and Lombardi, K. (1998) The unconscious catch in psychoanalytic supervision, in N. Rucker and K. Lombardi (eds) *Subject Relations: Unconscious Experience and Relational Psychoanalysis*. New York: Routledge.

Rychlak, J. F. (1997) *In Defense of Human Consciousness*. Washington, DC: American Psychological Association.

Safran, J. D. and Greenberg, L. S. (1987) Affect and the unconscious: a cognitive perspective, in R. Stern (ed.) *Theories of the Unconscious and Theories of the Self*. Hillsdale, NJ: Analytic Press.

Salkovskis, P. M. (ed.) (1996) *Frontiers of Cognitive Therapy*. New York: Guilford.

Schacter, D. L. (1996) *Searching for Memory: The Brain, the Mind and the Past*. New York: Basic Books.

Schultz, D. P. and Schultz, S. E. (2000) *A History of Modern Psychology*, 7th edn. Fort Worth, TX: Harcourt College Publishers.

Schwartz-Salant, N. (1995) On the interactive field as the analytic object, in M. Stein (ed.) *The Interactive Field in Analysis: Volume 1*. Wilmette, IL: Chiron.

Searles, H. F. (1955) The informational value of the supervisor's emotional experiences, in H. F. Searles (1965) *Collected Papers on Schizophrenia and Related Subjects*. London: Hogarth Press/Karnac Books.

Segal, Z. V., Williams, J. M. G. and Teasdale, J. D. (2002) *Mindfulness-based Cognitive Therapy for Depression: A New Approach to Preventing Relapse*. New York: Guilford.

Sheldrake, R. (1985) *A New Science of Life: The Hypothesis of Formative Causation*. London: Anthony Blond.

Sheldrake, R. (1989) *The Presence of the Past*. London: Fontana.

Sheldrake, R. (1992) *The Rebirth of Nature: The Greening of Science and God*. New York: Bantam.

Shirk, S. and Harter, S. (1996) Treatment of low self-esteem, in M. Reinecke, F. Dattilio and A. Freeman (eds) *Cognitive Therapy with Children and Adolescents: A Casebook for Clinical Practice*. New York: Guilford.

Singer, J. (1990) *Seeing through the Visible World: Jung, Gnosis and Chaos*. New York: Harper San Francisco.

Skinner, B. F. (1953) *Science and Human Behavior*. New York: Macmillan.

Smith, D. L. (1999a) Communicative psychotherapy without tears, in E. M. Sullivan (ed.) *Unconscious Communication in Practice*. Buckingham: Open University Press.

Smith, D. L. (1999b) Understanding patients' countertransferences, in E. M. Sullivan (ed.) *Unconscious Communication in Practice*. Buckingham: Open University Press.

Smith, H. (1964) Do drugs have religious import? In R. Walsh and F. Vaughan (eds) *Paths beyond Ego: The Transpersonal Vision*. Los Angeles: Jeremy P. Tarcher/Perigee (first published 1964).

Smucker, M. R. (1997) Post-traumatic stress disorder, in R. Leahy (ed.) *Practicing Cognitive Therapy: A Guide to Interventions*. Northvale, NJ: Jason Aronson.

Spanos, N. P., Menary, E., Gabora, N. J., DuBreuil, S. C. and Dewhirst, B. (1991) Secondary identity enactments during hypnotic past-life regression: a sociocognitive perspective, *Journal of Personality and Social Psychology*, 61: 308–20.

Sperry, R. W. (1995) The future of psychology, *American Psychologist*, 50: 505–6.

Spiegler, M. D. and Guevremont, D. C. (1998) *Contemporary Behavioral Therapy*, 3rd edn. Pacific Grove, CA: Brooks/Cole.

Stafford, P. (1992) *Psychedelics Encyclopedia*, 3rd edn. Berkeley, CA: Ronin.

Stein, D. (1997) Introduction: cognitive science and the unconscious, in D. Stein (ed.) *Cognitive Science and the Unconscious*. Washington, DC: American Psychiatric Press.

Stein, D. and Young, J. E. (1997) Rethinking repression, in D. Stein (ed.) *Cognitive Science and the Unconscious*. Washington, DC: American Psychiatric Press.

Stein, M. (1995) The field of sleep, in M. Stein (ed.) *The Interactive Field in Analysis: Volume 1*. Wilmette, IL: Chiron.

Stepansky, P. E. (1983) *In Freud's Shadow: Adler in Context*. Hillsdale, NJ: Analytic Press.

Stern, D. B. (1997) *Unformulated Experience: From Dissociation to Imagination in Psychoanalysis*. Hillsdale, NJ: Analytic Press.

Stolorow, R. D. and Atwood, G. E. (1999) Three realms of the unconscious, in S. A. Mitchell and L. Aron (eds) *Relational Psychoanalysis: The Emergence of a Tradition*. Hillsdale, NJ: Analytic Press.

Stricker, G. and Gold, J. R. (1993) *Comprehensive Handbook of Psychotherapy Integration*. New York: Plenum.

Sullivan, H. S. (1937) A note on the implications of psychiatry, the study of interpersonal relations, for investigations in the social sciences, *American Journal of Sociology*, 42: 848–61.

Sullivan, H. S. (1938) Psychiatry: introduction to the study of interpersonal relations, *Psychiatry*, 1: 121–34.

Sullivan, H. S. (1950) The illusion of personal individuality, *Psychiatry*, 13: 317–32.

Sullivan, H. S. (1953) *The Interpersonal Theory of Psychiatry*. New York: W. W. Norton.

Summers, F. L. (1999) *Transcending the Self: An Object Relations Model of Psychoanalytic Therapy*. Hillsdale, NJ: Analytic Press.

Swami Venkatesananda (1982) *Buddha: Daily Readings*. Elgin, South Africa: Chiltern Yoga Trust.

Tart, C. (1972) States of consciousness and state specific sciences, *Science*, 176: 1204–10.

Tart, C. (1986) *Waking up! Overcoming the Obstacles to Human Potential*. Boulder, CO: Shambhala.

Tart, C. (1992) *Transpersonal Psychologies: Perspectives on the Mind from Seven Great Spiritual Traditions*, 2nd edn. San Francisco: HarperSanFrancisco.

Taylor, J. G. (1999) *The Race for Consciousness*. Cambridge, MA: MIT Press.

Teasdale, J. D. (1996) Clinically relevant theory: Integrating clinical insight with cognitive science, in P. M. Salkovskis (ed.) *Frontiers of Cognitive Therapy*. New York: Guilford.

Thorpe, M. (1982) Psychodiagnostics in a Xhosa Zionist church, Master's thesis, Rhodes University, Grahamstown, South Africa.

Valle, R. S. (1989) The emergence of transpersonal psychology, in R. S. Valle and S. Halling (eds) *Existential-phenomenological Perspectives in Psychology: Exploring the Breadth of Human Experience*. New York: Plenum.

Walsh, R. (1977) Initial meditative experiences: part 1, *Journal of Transpersonal Psychology*, 9: 151–92.

Walsh, R. (1978) Initial meditative experiences: part 2, *Journal of Transpersonal Psychology*, 10: 1–29.

Walsh, R. (1990) *The Spirit of Shamanism*. Los Angeles: Tarcher.

Walsh, R. and Vaughan, F. (1993) *Paths beyond Ego: The Transpersonal Vision*. Los Angeles: Jeremy P. Tarcher/Perigee.

Washburn, M. (1988) *The Ego and the Dynamic Ground: A Transpersonal Theory of Human Development*. Albany, NY: SUNY Press.

Washburn, M. (1994) *Transpersonal Psychology in Psychoanalytic Perspective*. Albany, NY: SUNY Press.

Watkins, J. G. (1984) The Bianchi (LA Hillside Strangler) case: sociopath or multiple personality?, *International Journal of Clinical and Experimental Hypnosis*, 32: 67–101.

Watson, R. I. (1968) Janet, Pierre, in D. Sills (ed.) *International Encyclopedia of the Social Sciences, Volume 8*. New York: Macmillan.

Way, L. (1950) *Adler's Place in Psychology*. London: George Allen and Unwin.

Wehr, G. (1987) *Jung: A Biography*. Boston: Shambhala.

Weiskrantz, L. (1997) *Consciousness Lost and Found*. Oxford: Oxford University Press.

Wessler, R. L. and Hankin-Wessler, S. W. R. (1989) Nonconscious algorithms in cognitive and affective processes, *Journal of Cognitive Psychotherapy*, 3: 243–54.

Whyte, L. L. (1962) *The Unconscious before Freud*. London: Tavistock.

Wilber, K. (1975) Psychologia perennis: the spectrum of consciousness, *Journal of Transpersonal Psychology*, 2: 105–32.

Wilber, K. (1979) A developmental view of consciousness, *Journal of Transpersonal Psychology*, 11: 1–22.

Wilber, K. (1981a) Ontogenetic development: two fundamental patterns, *Journal of Transpersonal Psychology*, 13: 33–58.

Wilber, K. (1981b) *Up from Eden*. New York: Anchor/Doubleday.

Wilber, K. (1998) *The Marriage of Sense and Soul: Integrating Science and Religion*. New York: Random House.

Wilson, G. T. and O'Leary, K. D. (1980) *Principles of Behavior Therapy.* Englewood Cliffs, NJ: Prentice Hall.

Winnicott, D. W. (1965) Ego distortion in terms of true and false self, in *The Maturational Processes and the Facilitating Environment.* London: Hogarth Press.

Wolpe, J., Salter, A. and Reyna, L. J. (eds) (1964) *The Conditioning Therapies: The Challenge in Psychotherapy.* New York: Holt, Rinehart and Winston.

Wulff, D. M. (2000) Mystical experience, in E. Cardeña, S. J. Lynn and S. Krippner (eds) *The Varieties of Anomolous Experience.* Washington, DC: American Psychological Association.

Yontef, G. (1993) *Awareness, Dialogue and Process: Essays on Gestalt Therapy.* Highland, NY: Gestalt Journal Press.

Young, J. E. (1994) *Cognitive Therapy for Personality Disorders: A Schema-focused Approach,* 2nd edn. Sarasota, FL: Professional Resource Press.

Young, J. E. and Flanagan, C. (1998) Schema-focused therapy for narcissistic patients, in E. F. Ronningstam (ed.) *Disorders of Narcissism: Diagnostic, Clinical, and Empirical Implications.* Washington, DC: American Psychiatric Press.

Zajonc, R. B. (1980) Preferences need no inferences, *American Psychologist,* 35: 151–75.

Index

MODELS OF PSYCHOPATHOLOGY

Dilys Davies and Dinesh Bhugra

Models and theories of psychopathology and their associated clinical practice do not represent scientific fact so much as a variation in perspective within psychopathology itself. Several favoured models exist within any society at a given time, and as well as changing historically over time, they also differ culturally between societies.

This book examines:

- the similarities, differences and points of integration in the main models of psychopathology
- how the theoretical conceptualizations underpinning these models are reflected in the theory and the clinical practice of different schools of psychotherapy
- how various models are used in everyday practice
- whether clinicians adhere to the rules of a given model or whether, in fact, there is more integration in practice than there appears to be in theoretical conceptualizations.

Models of Psychopathology is aimed at advanced undergraduates and postgraduate students of clinical psychology, counselling psychology, psychotherapy and counselling. It will also be of interest to therapy students in professional training courses and experienced clinicians who want to know more about this aspect of psychotherapy.

Contents
Series editor's preface – Introduction – Descriptive models – Psychoanalytical model – Behavioural model – Cognitive model – Humanistic model – Social model – Critique from a socio-cultural view – Conclusion – References – Index.

128pp   0 335 20822 3 (Paperback)   0 335 20823 1 (Hardback)

EMOTIONS AND NEEDS

Dawn Freshwater and Chris Robertson

Through the centrality of the concepts of needs and emotions, this volume describes and discusses issues that are fundamental to psychotherapy. As an alternative to classifying modalities of psychotherapy (and the way in which they understand needs and emotions) by their author, era or underpinning philosophy, this book focuses instead on the emotional patterning of psychotherapy.

The book explores need and emotion in relation to what patients bring to therapy and what subsequently facilitates effective engagement. Examining ways of understanding the manifestation of needs and emotions, the authors bring differing therapeutic schools of thought together in contemporary models of integrative psychotherapy which draw upon the transpersonal, postmodern and post structural. The book is illustrated throughout with clinical vignettes, which help the reader ground the theoretical concepts in everyday practice.

The discussions in this volume not only add to the current body of knowledge of surrounding the fundamental concepts of emotions and needs, but also make a long overdue contribution to the psychotherapeutic professions. *Emotions and Needs* will be of interest to students and practitioners in fields such as: counselling, psychotherapy, clinical psychology and social work.

Contents
Series editor's preface – Preface – Needs and emotions – Emotional sources – The emotional encounter – Emotional distillation – Emotions and integration – References – Further reading – Index.

160pp   0 335 20801 0 (Paperback)   0 335 20802 9 (Hardback)

TRANSFERENCE AND PROJECTION
MIRRORS TO THE SELF

Jan Grant and Jim Crawley

This book describes, defines and demonstrates the clinical applications of transference and projection and how they are used by psychotherapists as 'mirrors to the self' – as reflections of a client's internal structure and core ways of relating to other people. There is an emphasis on understanding transference as a normal organizing process that helps individuals make meaning of interpersonal experiences. There is also a focus on how to respond effectively to transference and projection in the day-to-day practice of counselling and psychotherapy. Comprehensive coverage of the ways in which the major schools of psychotherapy understand and utilize such phenomena is also provided. Theoretical principles are illustrated by lively clinical anecdotes from the authors' own psychotherapy practices.

Transference and Projection is aimed at advanced undergraduate and postgraduate students of psychotherapy, counselling, counselling psychology and clinical psychology. It will also be of interest to therapy students in professional training courses and experienced clinicians who want to know more about this aspect of psychotherapy.

Contents
Series editor's preface – Preface – Mirrors to the self: an introduction to transference – Projection and projective identification – Early development of the understanding of transference – Developments in understanding transference: Psychodynamic psychotherapies – Schemas and scripts: cognitive-behavioural therapy and transference – The real relationship: transference and humanistic-existential/experiential therapies – The transference prism: couples and family therapy – Recognizing and responding to transference – References – Index.

176pp   0 335 20314 0 (Paperback)   0 335 20315 9 (Hardback)

BODY PSYCHOTHERAPY
AN INTRODUCTION

Nick Totton

Body psychotherapy is an holistic therapy which approaches human beings as united bodymind, and offers embodied relationship as its central therapeutic stance. Well-known forms include Reichian Therapy, Bioenergetics, Dance Movement Therapy, Primal Integration and Process Oriented Psychology.

This new title examines the growing field of body psychotherapy:

- Surveys the many forms of body psychotherapy
- Describes what may happen in body psychotherapy and offers a theoretical account of how this is valuable drawing in current neuro-scientific evidence
- Defines the central concepts of the field, and the unique skills needed by practitioners
- Accessible and practical, yet grounded throughout in current research

Body Psychotherapy: An Introduction is of interest to practitioners and students of all forms of psychotherapy and counselling, and anyone who wants to understand how mind and body together form a human being.

Contents
Introduction – What happens in body psychotherapy? – Foundations of body psychotherapy – Models, concepts and skills – Varieties of body psychotherapy – Clinical and ethical issues – The future of body psychotherapy – Resources – Bibliography – Index.

200pp   0 335 21038 4 (Paperback)   0 335 21039 2 (Hardback)